Workshop on Computational Approaches to Figurative Language 2007

Held at HLT/NAACL 2007

Rochester, New York, USA
26 April 2007

ISBN: 978-1-61738-514-8

Printed from e-media with permission by:

Curran Associates, Inc.
57 Morehouse Lane
Red Hook, NY 12571
www.proceedings.com

Some format issues inherent in the e-media version may also appear in this print version.

Printed by Curran Associates, Inc. (2010)

Association for Computational Linguistics
209 N. Eighth Street
Stroudsburg, Pennsylvania 18360

Phone: 1-570-476-8006
Fax: 1-570-476-0860

acl@aclweb.org

Introduction

Figurative language, such as metaphor, metonymy, idioms, personification, simile, among others, is in abundance in natural discourse. It is an effective apparatus to heighten effect and convey various meanings, such as humor, irony, sarcasm, affection, etc. Figurative language can be found not only in fiction, but also in everyday speech, newspaper articles, research papers, and even technical reports. The recognition of figurative language use and the computation of figurative language meaning constitute one of the hardest problems for a variety of natural language processing tasks, such as machine translation, text summarization, information retrieval, and question answering. Resolution of this problem involves both a solid understanding of the distinction between literal and non-literal language and the development of effective computational models that can make the appropriate semantic interpretation automatically.

The emphasis of this workshop is on computational approaches to figurative language, be it modeling or natural language processing. The goal of the workshop is to provide a venue for researchers to reach a better understanding of the new issues and challenges that need to be tackled in dealing with non-literal phenomena. We are very happy that the workshop has attracted people from different disciplines and hope that the workshop will continue to live in the future.

It is our pleasure to thank our invited speaker, Rada Mihalcea (of University of North Texas), for her presentation "The Language of Humor". We would also like to thank all the members of the program committee for their advice and for reviewing the papers carefully on a tight schedule. Enjoy the workshop!

Anna Feldman and Xiaofei Lu
Co-Chairs

Organizers:

Anna Feldman, Montclair State University
Xiaofei Lu, The Pennsylvania State University

Program Committee:

Chris Brew, The Ohio State University, USA
Paul Cook, University of Toronto, Canada
Afsaneh Fazly, University of Toronto, Canada
Eileen Fitzpatrick, Montclair State University, USA
Sam Glucksberg, Princeton University, USA
Sid Horton, Northwestern University, USA
Diana Inkpen, University of Ottawa, Canada
Kevin Knight, USC/Information Sciences Institute, USA
Mark Lee, The University of Birmingham, UK
Katja Markert, University of Leeds, UK
Detmar Meurers The Ohio State University, USA
Rada Mihalcea, University of North Texas, USA
Andrew Ortony, Northwestern University, USA
Wim Peters, University of Sheffield, UK
Vasile Rus, The University of Memphis, USA
Richard Sproat, University of Illinois at Urbana-Champain, USA
Suzanne Stevenson, University of Toronto, Canada
Carlo Strapparava, Istituto per la Ricerca Scientifica e Tecnologica, Italy

Invited Speaker:

Rada Mihalcea, University of North Texas, USA

Table of Contents

Lexical Influences on the Perception of Sarcasm
Roger Kreuz and Gina Caucci 1

Corpus-driven Metaphor Harvesting
Astrid Reining and Birte Lönneker-Rodman 5

Hunting Elusive Metaphors Using Lexical Resources
Saisuresh Krishnakumaran and Xiaojin Zhu 13

Active Learning for the Identification of Nonliteral Language
Julia Birke and Anoop Sarkar 21

Conference Program

Thursday, April 26, 2007

8:45–9:00 Opening Remarks

9:00–9:30 *Lexical Influences on the Perception of Sarcasm*
Roger Kreuz and Gina Caucci

9:30–10:00 *Corpus-driven Metaphor Harvesting*
Astrid Reining and Birte Lönneker-Rodman

10:00–10:30 *Hunting Elusive Metaphors Using Lexical Resources*
Saisuresh Krishnakumaran and Xiaojin Zhu

10:30–11:00 Break

11:00–11:30 *Active Learning for the Identification of Nonliteral Language*
Julia Birke and Anoop Sarkar

11:30–12:30 Invited Talk: The Language of Humor
Rada Mihalcea

Lexical Influences on the Perception of Sarcasm

Roger J. Kreuz
Department of Psychology
The University of Memphis
Memphis, TN 38152
rkreuz@memphis.edu

Gina M. Caucci
Department of Psychology
The University of Memphis
Memphis, TN 38152
gcaucci@memphis.edu

Abstract

Speakers and listeners make use of a variety of pragmatic factors to produce and identify sarcastic statements. It is also possible that lexical factors play a role, although this possibility has not been investigated previously. College students were asked to read excerpts from published works that originally contained the phrase *said sarcastically*, although the word *sarcastically* was deleted. The participants rated the characters' statements in these excerpts as more likely to be sarcastic than those from similar excerpts that did not originally contain the word *sarcastically*. The use of interjections, such as *gee* or *gosh*, predicted a significant amount of the variance in the participants' ratings of sarcastic intent. This outcome suggests that sarcastic statements may be more formulaic than previously realized. It also suggests that computer software could be written to recognize such lexical factors, greatly increasing the likelihood that nonliteral intent could be correctly interpreted by such programs, even if they are unable to identify the pragmatic components of nonliteral language.

1 Introduction

It has long been assumed that verbal irony, or sarcasm, is principally a pragmatic phenomenon, and many studies from psycholinguistics have demonstrated the social, contextual, and interpersonal factors that affect its use and interpretation (for reviews, see Gibbs, 1994, 2003; Giora, 2003).

An example of such a pragmatic factor is *common ground* (Clark, 1996). The more familiar two people are with one other, the more likely it is that they will employ sarcasm (Kreuz, 1996). When interlocutors in a story share common ground, experimental participants read sarcastic statements more quickly, and are more certain of the sarcastic intent, than when the interlocutors share little common ground (Kreuz and Link, 2002). These results can be explained in terms of a *principle of inferability*: speakers will only employ sarcasm if they are reasonably certain that their hearers will interpret it correctly (Kreuz, 1996).

Such results have led to pessimistic forecasts concerning the likelihood that computer programs would ever be able to understand nonliteral language (e.g., Dews and Winner, 1997). If the use of such language relies solely on pragmatic factors, it would indeed be a considerable challenge to create software that could detect and interpret it.

One difficulty with this conclusion is that most psycholinguistic studies of sarcasm have used experimenter-generated materials instead of actual utterances. For example, sarcastic statements are often hyperbolic (Kreuz and Roberts, 1995), and so researchers have typically employed extreme constructions, such as *What perfectly lovely weather!* as sarcastic commentary on a sudden downpour (Kreuz and Glucksberg, 1989).

Such research, however, has unintentionally confounded the *pragmatic* and the *lexical* aspects of sarcasm. It may be the case that particular words or collocations (e.g., *perfectly lovely*) serve as a cue

Proceedings of the Workshop on Computational Approaches to Figurative Language, pages 1–4,
Rochester, NY, April 26, 2007.

for sarcasm by themselves. Previous research has not attempted to tease apart these lexical and pragmatic factors, even though the importance of lexical factors has been suggested previously. Kreuz and Roberts (1995) proposed that collocations consisting of extreme adjectives and adverbs (e.g., *simply amazing*, or *absolutely fantastic*) may serve as a conventional way of signaling ironic intent. This idea has been expanded by Utsumi (2000), who suggested that such verbal cues provide a way of implicitly displaying negative attitudes via sarcasm.

Of course, interlocutors in face-to-face conversations can rely upon both verbal and nonverbal cues to signal ironic intent (e.g., rolling of the eyes, heavy stress, or slow speaking rate). The authors of narratives must cue their readers without recourse to such conventions. The methods used by authors, therefore, might provide a way to assess the contribution of lexical factors to the perception of sarcasm.

The goal of the present research was to determine whether specific lexical factors (e.g., the use of certain parts of speech, or punctuation) reliably predict readers' perceptions of sarcasm. Unlike most previous research on sarcasm, the experimental materials were drawn from published narratives.

2 Method

Participants were asked to read excerpts from longer narratives, and then to rate how likely it was that the speaker was being sarcastic.

2.1 Materials

Google Book Search was used to find instances of the phrase *said sarcastically*. This resource, formerly known as Google Print, contains more than 100,000 published works that are either in the public domain, or have been provided by publishers. A wide variety of genres is represented (e.g., historical novels, romance novels, and science fiction).

The phrase *said sarcastically* was found hundreds of times in the corpus, and 100 of these instances were randomly selected for the study. Fifteen control texts were also selected at random from the Google Book Search corpus. Five of the control items contained the phrase *I said*, five contained *he said*, and five contained *she said*.

In order to create experimental materials, we excerpted the entire paragraph that the key phrase appeared in, as well as the two paragraphs of context appearing above and below. The excerpts varied considerably in length, but the mean length for the 115 excerpts was 110 words ($SD = 58$).

The phrase that the collocation *said sarcastically* referred to was emphasized in bold-faced type. If the phrase appeared at the end of a sentence, only the words that occurred before it within quotation marks were made bold. If the sentence continued after the phrase *said sarcastically*, the following words in quotation marks were also made bold. Finally, the word *sarcastically* was removed, leaving just the phrase *[speaker] said*. The speakers' statements in the control excerpts were made bold using the same procedure, ensuring that the two sets of excerpts were identical in appearance. The mean length of the bold-faced phrases for all the excerpts was 6.45 words ($SD = 8.05$).

Each excerpt was printed on a separate page, along with three questions. The first question asked *How likely is it that the speaker was being sarcastic?* A seven-point scale, with endpoints labeled *not at all likely* and *very likely*, appeared below the question. A second question asked *Why do you think so?* Two blank lines were provided for the participants' responses. Finally, the participants were asked *How certain are you that the speaker was being sarcastic?* A seven-point scale, with endpoints labeled *not at all certain* and *very certain*, appeared below the question.

Five different sets of sarcasm excerpts (20 per set) were created. Booklets were constructed by randomly interspersing the subset of sarcasm excerpts with all of the control excerpts. The order of pages was randomized for each participant.

2.2 Coding

Two judges independently coded the excerpts on three dimensions:

(1) **Presence of adjectives and adverbs.** Following Kreuz and Roberts (1995) and Utsumi (2000), the judges identified the use of adjectives or adverbs in the bold-faced segments of each excerpt. The coding was binary: 0 for none, and 1 for one or more adjectives and adverbs.

(2) **Presence of interjections.** Certain terms, such as *gee* or *gosh*, are used for the expression of emotion, and may also serve as a cue for nonliteral

intent. The excerpts were again coded in a binary fashion.

(3) **Use of punctuation**. Exclamation points indicate emphasis, which may be a signal of nonliteral intent. Question marks are used in tag questions (e.g., *You really showed him, didn't you?*), which are often rhetorical and nonliteral (Kreuz et al., 1999). The use of either an exclamation point or question mark was coded in a binary fashion.

The agreement between the judges' coding was 95% across all excerpts. The small number of disagreements was primarily the result of variability in how dictionaries define interjections. All disagreements were resolved through discussion.

2.3 Procedure

Participants were 101 undergraduates at a large public university. They received course credit for their participation. The participants were tested in small groups, and asked to work through the booklets at their own pace. Each participant read and answered questions for 35 excerpts: 20 sarcasm excerpts, and all 15 control excerpts (only a subset of the sarcasm materials was given to each participant to offset fatigue effects).

The term *sarcasm* was not defined for the participants, and they were asked to rely solely on their intuitive understanding of the term. (Previous research with the same population suggests that a fairly high level of agreement exists for the concept of sarcasm; see Kreuz, Dress, and Link, 2006).

3 Results

Only the responses from the first question (likelihood that the speaker is being sarcastic) will be discussed here. For each participant, a mean score for the 100 sarcasm and 15 control excerpts was computed. As expected, the sarcasm excerpts received higher scores ($M = 4.85$, $SD = .67$) than the control excerpts ($M = 2.89$, $SD = .86$), and the difference was significant, $t\ (100) = 19.35$, $p < .001$. This means that the participants had sufficient context for determining sarcastic intent in the test excerpts, and that the participants were able to distinguish between the two groups of excerpts.

To determine the relative importance of the lexical factors on the perception of sarcasm, a regression analysis was performed. The criterion variable was the mean sarcasm rating for each excerpt. Five predictor variables were employed: (1) the number of words in each excerpt, (2) the number of bold-faced words in each excerpt, (3) the presence of adjectives and adverbs, (4) the presence of interjections, and (5) the use of exclamation points and question marks. Variables 3 to 5 were coded in a binary fashion, as described in section 2.2. Ratings for both the sarcastic and the control excerpts were entered.

The number of words and number of bold-faced words are theoretically uninteresting variables, so they were forced into the equation first as one block. The three predictor variables of interest were entered in a second block using a stepwise method.

The first block, containing the two length variables, failed to account for a significant amount of the variance, $F\ (2,112) = 1.37$, *n.s.*, $R^2 = .024$. This was a desirable outcome, because it meant that participants were not influenced in their judgments by the lengths of the excerpts they were reading, with longer excerpts providing more contextual cues.

For the second block with the three variables of interest, only the presence of interjections entered into the equation, $F\ (1, 111) = 6.10$, $p = .015$, $R^2 = .051$. The presence of adjectives and adverbs, and the use of punctuation, failed to predict a significant amount of the variance in the participants' ratings of sarcastic intent.

4 Discussion

Previous theory and research has largely ignored the potential role of lexical factors in the delivery and detection of sarcasm. This bias has been reinforced by the use of experimenter-generated materials that may have obscured the contributions made by these factors. This study is the first to assess the importance of such lexical factors, using ecologically valid materials.

On the one hand, the amount of variance accounted for by lexical factors was rather small: just 5%. On the other hand, it must be remembered that the excerpts themselves were taken from book-length works, so the participants only had a fraction of the original context with which to determine the intent of the (potentially) sarcastic statement. Nevertheless, the participants were able to reliably differentiate between the sarcastic and control excerpts, which suggests that specific local factors were influencing their judgments.

In addition, it must be remembered that only a small number of lexical factors was assessed, and in a fairly coarse way (i.e., with binary coding). Out of just three such factors, however, the use of interjections was a significant predictor of the participants' ratings. An inspection of the excerpts suggests that certain formulaic expressions (e.g., *thanks a lot*, *good job*), foreign terms (e.g., *au contraire*), rhetorical statements (e.g., *tell us what you really think*), and repetitions (e.g., *perfect, just perfect*) are also common in sarcastic statements. However, the set of excerpts was not large enough to allow an analysis of these expressions. A large online corpus would permit the identification of many such collocations, but determining whether the phrases were actually intended sarcastically would be more difficult than in the present study.

One could argue that the use of the phrase *said sarcastically* reflects poorly on the authors themselves. Ideally, a writer would not need to be so explicit about a character's intentions: it should be clear from the context that the statement was intended nonliterally. However, an author is writing for an indeterminate audience that may exist in the present or in some future time. It should not be surprising, therefore, that authors occasionally feel the need to use such a phrase, and this reflects how difficult it is to communicate nonliteral intent clearly.

It should also be noted, however, that some of the authors used the word *sarcastically* rather broadly, as a synonym for *angrily* or *jokingly*, even when the statement was intended literally. This suggests that the use of this term may be undergoing some change (see Nunberg, 2001 for a similar claim).

Finally, these results have important implications for software programs that attempt to "understand" natural language. Nonliteral language presents formidable challenges for such programs, since a one-to-one mapping of words to meaning will not lead to a correct interpretation (e.g., *Gee, I just love spending time waiting in line*). However, the present results suggest that, in some contexts, the use of interjections, and perhaps other textual factors, may provide reliable cues for identifying sarcastic intent.

References

Herbert H. Clark, 1996. *Using Language*. Cambridge: Cambridge University Press.

Shelly Dews and Ellen Winner, 1997. Attributing meaning to deliberately false utterances: The case of irony. In C. Mandell and A. McCabe (Eds.), *The Problem of Meaning: Behavioral and Cognitive Perspectives*. Amsterdam: Elsevier.

Raymond W. Gibbs, Jr., 1994. *The Poetics of Mind: Figurative Thought, Language, and Understanding*. Cambridge: Cambridge University Press.

Raymond W. Gibbs, Jr., 2003. Nonliteral speech acts in text and discourse. In A. C. Graesser, M. A. Gernsbacher, and S. R. Goldman (Eds.), *Handbook of Discourse Processes* (pp. 357-393). Mahwah, NJ: Lawrence Erlbaum Associates.

Rachel Giora, 2003. *On our Mind: Salience, Context, and Figurative Language*. New York: Oxford University Press.

Roger J. Kreuz, 1996. The use of verbal irony: Cues and constraints. In J. S. Mio and A. N. Katz (Eds.), *Metaphor: Implications and Applications* (pp. 23-38). Mahwah, NJ: Lawrence Erlbaum Associates

Roger J. Kreuz, Megan L. Dress, and Kristen E. Link, 2006, July. *Regional Differences in the Spontaneous Use of Sarcasm*. Paper presented at the annual meeting of the Society for Text and Discourse, Minneapolis, MN.

Roger J. Kreuz and Sam Glucksberg, 1989. How to be sarcastic: The echoic reminder theory of verbal irony. *Journal of Experimental Psychology: General*, 118:374-386.

Roger J. Kreuz, Max A. Kassler, Lori Coppenrath, and Bonnie McLain Allen, 1999. Tag questions and common ground effects in the perception of verbal irony. *Journal of Pragmatics*, 31:1685-1700.

Roger J. Kreuz and Kristen E. Link, 2002. Asymmetries in the use of verbal irony. *Journal of Language and Social Psychology*, 21:127-143.

Roger J. Kreuz and Richard M. Roberts, 1995. Two cues for verbal irony: Hyperbole and the ironic tone of voice. *Metaphor and Symbolic Activity*, 10:21-31.

Geoffrey Nunberg, 2001. *The Way we Talk Now: Commentaries on Language and Culture*. Boston: Houghton Mifflin

Akira Utsumi, 2000. Verbal irony as implicit display of ironic environment: Distinguishing ironic utterances from nonirony. *Journal of Pragmatics*, 32:1777-1806.

Corpus-driven Metaphor Harvesting

Astrid Reining
Institute of Romance Languages
University of Hamburg
20146 Hamburg, Germany
astrid.reining@uni-hamburg.de

Birte Lönneker-Rodman
International Computer Science Institute
1947 Center Street, Suite 600
Berkeley, CA 94704, USA
loenneke@icsi.berkeley.edu

Abstract

The paper presents a corpus-based method for finding metaphorically used lexemes and prevailing semantico-conceptual source domains, given a target domain corpus. It is exemplified by a case study on the target domain of European politics, based on a French 800,000 token corpus.

1 Introduction

This investigation is situated within the framework of the Hamburg Metaphor Database[1] (HMD) (Lönneker and Eilts, 2004), which collects manual annotations of metaphors in context. HMD annotation terminology refers to cognitive linguistic accounts of metaphor. These suggest that abstract "target" concepts are often thought and talked of in terms of less abstract "source" concepts (Section 2). On these accounts, the paper presents a method for finding metaphorically used lexical items and characterizing the conceptual source domains they belong to, given a target domain corpus.

After mentioning related work on metaphor annotation (Section 3), we exemplify our method by a case study on the target domain of European politics, for which a French 800,000 token corpus is prepared and imported into a corpus manager (Section 4). Using corpus manager functions, a small set of highly salient collocates of *Europe* are classified as candidates of metaphorical usages; after assessing their metaphoricity in context, these lexemes are grouped into semantico-conceptual domains for which, in a final step, additional lexical instantiations are searched (Section 5). Two important source domains (BUILDING and MOTION) are detected, which are supported by over 1,000 manual corpus annotations. The domains can be characterized as small networks of EuroWordNet synsets (nodes) and lexical as well as conceptual relations (Section 6). Section 7 concludes the paper.

[1] http://www1.uni-hamburg.de/metaphern

2 Theoretical Aspects

The Conceptual Theory of Metaphor (CTM) worked out originally by (Lakoff and Johnson, 1980) claims that conceptual metaphors such as GOOD IS UP and TIME IS MONEY structure the way we think and influence the way we use language. Conceptual metaphors are mappings between conceptual domains, for example between the target domain GOOD and the less abstract source domain UP, or between TIME (target) and MONEY (source).

Conceptual metaphors are rarely *directly* referred to in speech or writing: Whereas *time is money* is a standing expression in English, this is much less so for many other conceptual mappings (cf. *?good is up*). Consequently, corpus analysis cannot have as a goal finding conceptual mappings as such. Rather, it can find their manifestations through non-literal usages of lexical items – i.e., contexts in which source domain words are used to refer to elements in the target domain.

For example, *high* (a word from the UP source domain) means 'good' in the expression *high marks*; and *spend* or *save*, used in the source domain to refer to actions involving money, refer to actions in the

Proceedings of the Workshop on Computational Approaches to Figurative Language, pages 5–12,
Rochester, NY, April 26, 2007.

target domain of TIME when used in contexts such as *spend time* or *save time*.

Adopting a broad notion of metaphor based on CTM, we refer to such non-literal usages (though often conventionalized) as *lexical metaphors* in this paper. Prominent conceptual metaphors are illustrated by a larger number of lexical metaphors, which support the systematicity of their mapping.

3 Related Work

Earlier projects annotating metaphor in corpora include (Martin, 1994) and (Barnden et al., 2002). In what follows, we give two examples of recent work.

Gedigian et al. (2006) annotated a subset of the *Wall Street Journal* for the senses of verbs from Motion-related, Placing, and Cure frames which were extracted from FrameNet (Fillmore et al., 2003). The annotation shows that more than 90% of the 4,186 occurrences of these verbs in the corpus data are lexical metaphors in the above sense. Gedigian et al. (2006) conclude that in the domain of economics, Motion-related metaphors are used conventionally to describe market fluctuations and policy decisions. A classifier trained on the annotated corpus can discriminate between literal and metaphorical usages of the verbs.

Lee (2006) compiled a 42,000 word corpus of transcribed doctor-patient dialogues, exhaustively hand-annotated for stretches of metaphorical language. These are provided with conceptual labels enabling the author to identify prevalent and interrelated metaphorical mappings used as part of communicative strategies in this domain.

4 The European Constitution Corpus

Exploration and annotation of a corpus to find information regarding its predominant conceptual source domains is most productive when applied to an abstract and novel target domain. Abstractness calls for ways to make the topic cognitively accessible, and novelty entails a certain openness about the particular source domains that might be activated for this purpose.

Abstractness and novelty are criteria fulfilled by the target domain selected for our study: European Constitutional politics. The domain is represented by the public discourse on the possible introduction of a European Constitution and on the corresponding French referendum (29 May 2005). The referendum allowed voters to accept or refuse the proposed Constitution text (the result being refusal). The remainder of this section describes the sources of the corpus (4.1), its acquisition (4.2), and pre-processing (4.3).

4.1 Sources

The corpus consists of two sub-corpora, collected from online versions of two French dailies, *Le Monde* and *Le Figaro*. The site `lemonde.fr` contains each article published in the printed version of the socialist-liberal newspaper *Le Monde*, whereas `lefigaro.fr` contains articles from the conservative newspaper *Le Figaro*.

4.2 Collection

From 27 April to 5 June, 2005, the above mentioned web sites were screened for articles on Europe and the European Constitution on a daily basis. For the case study presented in this paper, only articles dealing with the Constitution and discussing the referendum are retained. Each of these articles is a document of the European Constitution corpus and contains information on its publication date, author, and newspaper section (e.g. editorial). The selection of relevant articles is performed manually. This is labor-intensive but keeps noise to a minimum. As a guideline for distinguishing between "general" European topics and the referendum on the European Constitution, key words including *(European) Constitution* and *referendum* are used.

4.3 Preprocessing

The collected documents are converted into text format and annotated with a simple SGML tagset representing document meta data (in the header), paragraph boundaries, and sentence boundaries. Sentence detection is performed reusing TreeTagger scripts[2] because we POS-tag and lemmatize the texts using the TreeTagger (Schmid, 1994) and its French parameter file (Stein and Schmid, 1995). Finally, the corpus is verticalized for use with the Manatee/Bonito corpus manager (Rychlý and Smrž,

[2]Tokenizer perl script for modern French, available on Achim Stein's web page, `http://www.uni-stuttgart.de/lingrom/stein/forschung/resource.html` [accessed 4 September 2006].

2004), run in single platform mode on a Linux computer.

Table 1 gives an overview of the two sub-corpora. When collecting the corpus, relevance to the topic had been our only criterion. Interestingly, the two newspaper corpora are very similar in size. This means that the selected topic was assigned equal importance by the different newspaper teams. Tables 2 and 3 show absolute frequencies of the top ten lemmas, filtered by a list of 725 French stop words[3] but still including *oui* - 'yes' and *non* - 'no', buzz-words during the political debate on the European Constitution. The frequent words also give an impression of the domain centeredness of the corpus.

	Le Monde	Le Figaro
Size (tokens)	411,066	396,791
Distinct word forms	23,112	23,516
Distinct lemmas	13,093	13,618
Documents	410	489
Paragraphs	7,055	6,175
Subdocuments	59	n.a.
Sentences	17,421	17,210

Table 1: Size of the European Constitution corpus.

5 Lexical Metaphors and Source Domains

Our aim is to determine empirically salient metaphorical source domains used in the target domain of European politics, combined with the practical interest in speeding up the detection and annotation of lexical metaphors. In Subsection 3 above, two approaches to corpus annotation for metaphor were mentioned. Due to the size of the corpus and limited annotator resources, we cannot follow the full-text annotation approach adopted by Lee (2006). Neither do we proceed as Gedigian et al. (2006), because that approach pre-selects source domains and lemmas. In our approach, we search for metaphorically used lexical items from initially unknown source domains, so interesting lemmas cannot be listed *a priori*.

Therefore, we developed a new method which makes efficient use of existing corpus manager functions. The only constant is the representation of the target domain, predefined at a high level by the selection of our corpus. We fixed the lemma *Europe*

	Lemma	Occurrences
1.	*européen* - 'European'	2,033
2.	*non* - 'no'	2,306
3.	*Europe* - 'Europe'	1,568
4.	*politique* - 'political; politics'	1,159
5.	*oui* - 'yes'	1,124
6.	*France* - 'France'	1,110
7.	*constitution* - 'Constitution'	1,099
8.	*traité* - 'treaty'	906
9.	*monsieur* - 'mister'	872
10.	*mai* - 'May'	781

Table 2: Frequent words in the *Monde* sub-corpus.

	Lemma	Occurrences
1.	*européen* - 'European'	2,148
2.	*non* - 'no'	1,690
3.	*Europe* - 'Europe'	1,646
4.	*France* - 'France'	1,150
5.	*politique* - 'political; politics'	969
6.	*constitution* - 'Constitution'	921
7.	*oui* - 'yes'	917
8.	*ministre* - 'minister'	885
9.	*traité* - 'treaty'	856
10.	*devoir* - 'have to; obligation'	817

Table 3: Frequent words in the *Figaro* sub-corpus.

as a low-level anchor of the target domain.[4] The investigation proceeds in three steps:

1. Statistically weighted lists of collocates of the target domain lemma *Europe* are calculated and screened for candidates of metaphorical language use (5.1).

2. For the obtained candidate collocates, the corpus is concordanced in order to discriminate usages and assign a source domain to each collocate (5.2).

3. The source domains are extended lexically, making use of EuroWordNet synsets and relations (5.3).

Corpus data drives the discovery of relevant lemmas in step 1. In steps 2 and 3, the corpus is used to increasingly refine and evaluate findings regarding relevant lemmas and source domains.

5.1 Collocate analysis

At this stage, it is necessary to set a range (span) within which candidate lemmas are to appear, mea-

[3]Developed by Jean Véronis: `http://www.up.univ-mrs.fr/veronis/data/antidico.txt` [accessed 4 September 2006].

[4]We could have started with a larger set of target domain lemmas, e.g. *européen* - 'European', *Bruxelles* - 'Brussels', *UE* - 'EU' etc. However, the results for *Europe* quickly proved to be sufficient in number and variety to illustrate the method.

sured in lemma counts starting with the anchor word *Europe*. Sample concordances show that *Europe* is often preceded by an article and sometimes by an additional preposition. Based on this insight, we heuristically restrict the context range for collocates to four (i.e. three words are allowed to occur between it and *Europe*). For example, *mère* 'mother' in Example (1) is retained as a collocate:

(1) Parce qu'elle a été la **mère**$_4$ fondatrice$_3$ de$_2$ l$_1$'**Europe** unie. ('Because she [i.e. France] has been the founding mother of the unified Europe.')

The minimum absolute frequency of the collocate within the specified context range is set to 3, which ensures results of at least three example sentences per co-occurring lemma. Intentionally, no restriction is applied to the part of speech of the collocate.

For both sub-corpora, lists of the top 100 collocate lemmas for *Europe* are calculated in the Manatee/Bonito corpus manager. We use the MI-score for ranking; it is based on the relative frequency of the co-occurring lemmas. Choosing MI-score over T-score is driven by an interest in salient collocates of *Europe*, whether or not they are common in the entire corpus. (T-score would tend to prefer collocates that occur frequently throughout the corpus.) The top collocates and their MI-scores are given in Tables 4 and 5.

MI-scores of the 100 top-ranked collocates are between 7.297 and 4.575 in the *Monde* corpus and between 7.591 and 4.591 in the *Figaro* corpus. Empirically, a threshold of $MI >= 6$ retains the most salient collocates of *Europe* in both corpora. These

	Lemma	**MI**	**Abs. f**
1.	*panne* - 'breakdown'	7.297	6
2.	*uni* - 'unified'	7.275	13
3.	*réveil* - 'awakening; alarm clock'	7.034	3
4.	*unification* - 'unification'	6.864	4
5.	*paradoxe* - 'paradox'	6.812	3
6.	*construire* - 'construct'	6.799	31
7.	*résolument* - 'decidedly'	6.619	3
8.	*otage* - 'hostage'	6.619	3
9.	*utopie* - 'utopia'	6.619	3
10.	*défier* - 'defy, challenge'	6.619	3
...	...	...	...
26.	*révolte* - 'revolt'	6.034	3
...	...	...	...
100.	*maintenant* - 'now'	4.575	6

Table 4: Collocates of *Europe* in *Le Monde*.

	Lemma	**MI**	**Abs. f**
1.	*oriental* - 'oriental, east'	7.591	8
2.	*unifier* - 'unify'	7.498	6
3.	*Forum* - 'Forum'	7.176	3
4.	*occidental* - 'occidental, west'	7.065	5
5.	*panne* - 'breakdown'	6.913	8
6.	*ouest* - 'west'	6.691	3
7.	*prospère* - 'prosperous'	6.591	4
8.	*bouc* - 'goat'	6.498	3
9.	*patrie* - 'fatherland, home country'	6.498	3
10.	*ruine* - 'ruin'	6.498	3
...	...	...	...
20.	*doter* - 'endow'	6.006	8
...	...	...	...
100.	*attacher* - 'attach'	4.591	3

Table 5: Collocates of *Europe* in *Le Figaro*.

are 26 collocate lemmas from *Le Monde* and 20 from *Le Figaro*.

These highly salient collocates are evaluated for the potential of being used metaphorically in the target domain. The guideline underlying this evaluation is as follows: Those lexemes which, in at least one of their usages, designate entities belonging to domains more concrete than POLITICS (for example, BUILDING or FAMILY) are likely to be used metaphorically in the corpus. Specifically, among those collocates with $MI >= 6$, we identify the following metaphor candidates:

Le Monde *panne* - 'breakdown', *réveil* - 'awakening; alarm clock', *construire* - 'construct', *otage* - 'hostage', *bâtir* - 'build', *mère* - 'mother', *révolte* - 'revolt';

Le Figaro *panne*, *bouc* - 'goat', *ruine* - 'ruin', *traverser* - 'traverse', *racine* - 'root', *visage* - 'face', *reconstruire* - 'reconstruct'.

Merging the lists yields 13 distinct candidate words, which are now evaluated based on contexts from within the corpus. There are a total of 112 occurrences of these lemmas co-occurring with *Europe* in a range of 4, the setting used to calculate collocate lists. Each of them is inspected in a context of at least one sentence. An annotator decides whether the usage is metaphorical, and confirms this in almost all of the cases (cf. Table 6).

5.2 Source domain identification

While disambiguating the 13 candidate lemmas in context, the annotator also assigns a source domain

	Monde	Figaro	Total	Metaphor
construire	31	13	44	44
reconstruire	0	3	3	3
bâtir	5	1	6	6
ruine	0	3	3	0 or 3
panne	5	7	12	12
traverser	2	7	9	9
mère	3	1	4	4
racine	2	5	7	7
visage	2	5	7	7
réveil	3	0	3	3
révolte	3	0	3	3
otage	3	2	5	5
bouc	3	3	6	6
Total	62	50	112	109 or 112

Table 6: Co-occurrences of candidate lemmas.

label to each occurrence. Actually, to hold the status of source domain in a conceptual mapping, a conceptual domain should be instantiated systematically by a number of lexical metaphors. Therefore, as long as this systematicity has not been verified, the assigned source domains are tentative.

Four tentative source domains are postulated, two of which might need to be split into subdomains. The general domains are BUILDING, MOTION, FIGHT, and LIVING BEING. Verbs *(.V)* and nouns *(.N)* instantiating them are listed in Table 7. The table also contains further (though still ambiguous) lemmas from the Top-100 collocate list supporting the source domains. Observations regarding the source domains, based on the 112 annotated lexical metaphors, are summarized in what follows.

The BUILDING source domain has the highest number of lexical metaphor instantiations. The ambiguity of *ruine* - 'ruin', however, is unresolvable: The texts talk about "ruins of Europe" after World War II; if understood as "ruins of cities/buildings in Europe," all of these occurrences are literal, but if interpreted as "ruins of the European political system," all of them are metaphorical. The ambiguity might be deliberate.

	Domain	Disambiguated Lemmas	Futher collocates (Top 100)
1.	BUILDING	*construire.V*, *reconstruire.V*, *bâtir.V*, *ruine.N ?*	*maison.N* - 'house', *fonder.V* - 'found'
2.	MOTION		
	– FORWARD MOTION	*panne.N*, *traverser.V*	*progresser.V* - 'progress', *avancer.V* - 'advance'
	– MOTOR VEHICLE	*panne.N*	*moteur.N* - 'motor'
3.	FIGHT	*otage.N*, *révolte.N*	*lutter.V* - 'fight'
4.	LIVING BEING		
	– PROCREATION	*mère.N*, *racine.N*	*père.N* - 'father', *naître.V* - 'be born'
	– BODY	*visage.N*	*dos.N* - 'back', *coeur.N* - 'heart'
	– REST	*réveil.N*	–

Table 7: Tentative source domains.

Also the MOTION domain has been assigned to a large number of disambiguated occurrences. The noun *panne* - 'breakdown' might instantiate a subdomain, such as (MOTION IN A) MOTORIZED VEHICLE; in some cases, it has been assigned MACHINE as source domain, purposely underspecified as to its motion-relatedness.

The LIVING BEING source domain is multifaceted, comprising PROCREATION, BODY, and REST, obviously personifying Europe. However, the frequency of lexical metaphors in these domains is in large part due to recurring quotations: For example, *mère* - 'mother' is used exclusively within the expression *la mère fondatrice de l'Europe* - 'the founding mother of Europe,' attributed to J. L. Rodriguez Zapatero; and *réveil* - 'awakening; alarm clock' (pointing to an action of a living being) occurs only as part of the expression *sonner le réveil de l'Europe* - 'ring the awakening/alarm of Europe,' coined by Ph. de Villiers. Finally, *bouc* - 'goat' is always part of the idiom *le bouc émissaire* - 'scapegoat'. Although it could be grouped under LIVING BEING, this expression is based on particular cultural knowledge rather than on systematic exploitation of general world knowledge about the source domain.

The FIGHT domain has the lowest count of lexical metaphors in the annotated co-occurrences of *Europe*. Also, the noun *otage* - 'hostage' occurs three times out of five within the expression *(ne pas) prendre l'Europe en otage* - '(not) take Europe hostage,' coined by N. Sarkozy and quoted as such.

To summarize, we observe that the most salient lexical metaphors co-occurring with *Europe* in the European Constitution corpus either refer to the source domains of BUILDING or MOTION, well-known source domains of conventional metaphors, or the lexical metaphors are sparse, referring to much less clearly delimited source domains such as LIVING BEING or FIGHT. Within the second group, there are a number of newly coined expressions, "one shot rich image metaphors," (Lakoff, 1987) which evoke entire scenes but do not necessarily contribute to a wide-spread systematic exploitation of the source domain.

5.3 Lexical extension

Corpus annotation is now extended to a larger list of lemmas from the source domains of BUILDING and MOTION. The challenge here is finding additional lemmas that might exploit the postulated mappings, given a small set of disambiguated lemmas and ambiguous collocates (cf. Table 7). A lexical resource for French containing information on conceptual domains would be helpful here. EuroWordNet (EWN) could go in this direction. It defines many relation types, including the synonym relation inside synsets, as well as hyponym, near-antonym and meronym relations between synsets. Apart from these lexical relations, EWN also recognizes a family of semantico-conceptual INVOLVED relations, which relate a verb synset Y to a noun synset X if "X is the one/that who/which is *typically* involved in Ying" (Vossen, 1999) (our emphasis). Unfortunately, there are almost no actual instantiations of INVOLVED relations in the French part of EWN.

Taking our previously identified collocates of *Europe* as seeds, we extend our lemma list resorting to EuroWordNet synsets, as follows:

- lemmas in synsets lexically related by EWN relations to synsets containing our seed lemmas (hypo-, hyper-, anto-, mero- and synonyms);
- lemmas in synsets lexically related across part of speech to synsets containing our seed lemmas, by adding missing XPOS_NEAR_SYNONYM and XPOS_NEAR_ANTONYM relations ourselves;
- lemmas in synsets that are conceptually related to the seed synsets, by adding INVOLVED relations ourselves.

A reiteration of these steps (using encountered lemmas as new seeds) could lead very soon to general or peripheral lemmas. Ideally, one would set up a limit of reiteration per operation and consider all encountered lemmas as possible keywords of the domain. However, annotator resources being limited, we reduced the list of key lemmas to about 20 per domain (22 for BUILDING and 19 for MOTION), using human judgment.

At this stage, the restriction on the keyword of being a collocate of *Europe* is lifted. This results in search, disambiguation, and annotation being performed on *the entire corpus*. The annotator finds 663 lexical metaphors among the 1,237 occurrences of 22 BUILDING keywords, and 409 lexical metaphors among the 1,307 occurrences of 19 MOTION keywords. Each key lemma contributes positively to the count of lexical metaphors. Two consequences follow from these figures:

1. Both postulated source domains are systematically exploited by lexical metaphors.
2. Every second or third investigated occurrence is a lexical metaphor.[5] Collection and annotation of metaphors can thus proceed considerably faster on the key lemmas than it would on full text or randomly selected sentences.

For each lexical metaphor, the annotator provides EuroWordNet synset information. For the actual meaning in context, the synset belonging to the target domain is encoded. Additionally, the synset containing the metaphorically used lexeme *in its source domain sense* is indicated ("source synset").

6 Source domain structure

The information on source synsets underlies conceptual maps of the two source domains. This is exemplified here by Figure 1, which represents the MOTION domain. Lexical metaphors are prefixed by M_; those word senses not encoded in EWN are marked with an asterisk at the end. Synsets shaded gray in Figure 1 contain at least one lemma that is exploited as a lexical metaphor, and as such attested in the European Constitution corpus. Ovals represent verb synsets, boxes show noun synsets, and hexagons depict events.

Relations between synsets illustrate the internal structure of the domain. Solid lines represent relations encoded in EuroWordNet. For legibility reasons, labels of hyponym relations have been omitted.

[5] In the vicinity of *Europe*, the ratio continues to be higher, with at least three quarters of the contexts being metaphorical.

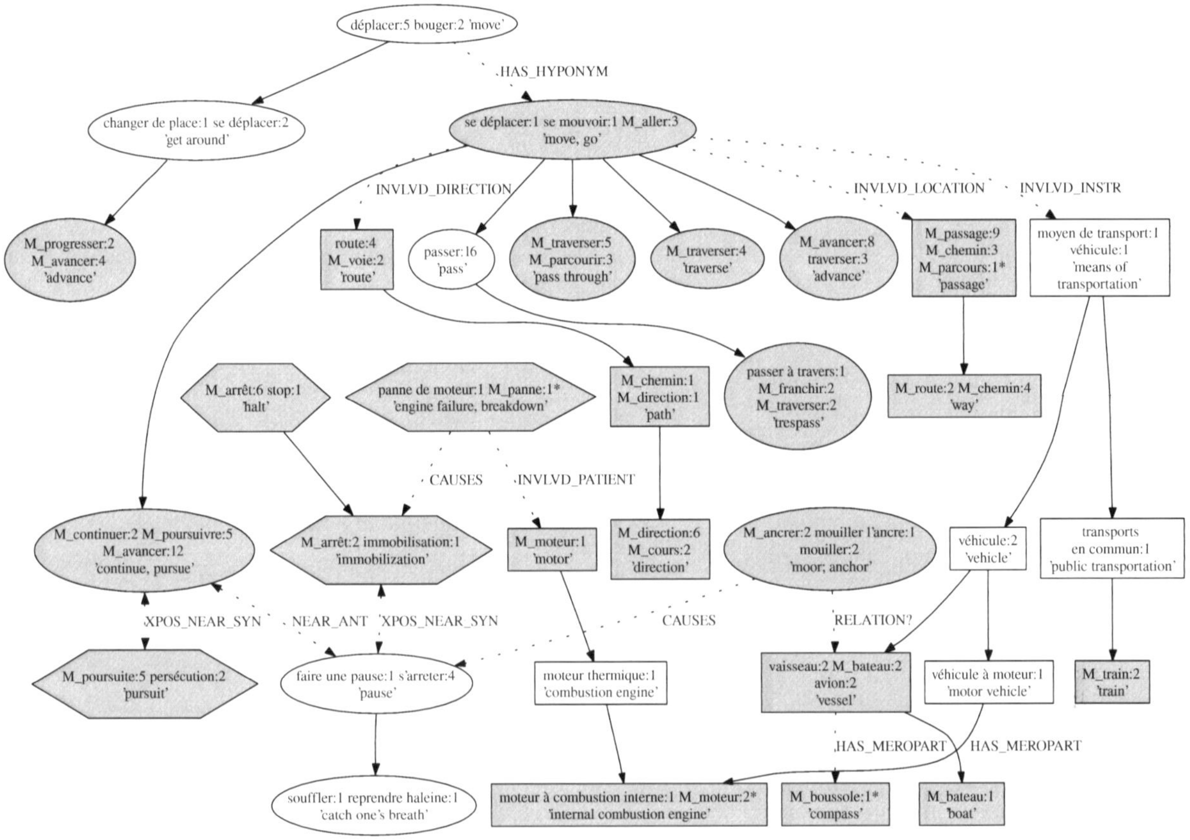

Figure 1: The MOTION source domain with corpus-specific highlights.

Dotted lines stand for relations that we added. These were labeled using EWN relation types (Vossen, 1999), where possible. As obvious from Figure 1, the domain graph would be separate partitions without our additional relations, especially those of the INVOLVED type. Conceptual relations ("typically...") are thus a necessary addition to lexical relations ("necessarily...") in order to represent conceptual source domains.

The map representing the source domain is a result of our corpus investigation of this specific target domain corpus. The structure of the source domain is not intended to be a general representation of this domain, nor does it imply fixed domain boundaries. Rather, the network shows the elements of the source domain that mapped onto the target domain from corpus attestations. If the same source domain were to be mapped onto some other target domain, other synsets might be used. A lexico-conceptual resource encoding general information on this source domain would thus have to contain more synsets and relations than those displayed in Figure 1.

The choice of source domains as well as of certain lexical items from within a source domain has the effect of "highlighting and hiding" certain aspects of the target domain. For example, among the numerous hyponyms of the central 'move' synset {*se déplacer:1 se mouvoir:1 aller:3*}–most of which are not displayed in Figure 1–, the European Constitution corpus shows a tendency towards lexical metaphors in synsets containing the verb *traverser* - 'traverse'. This profiles the path component of the motion event. The path itself is further emphasized by lexical metaphors related to the 'move' synset by INVOLVED_LOCATION and INVOLVED_DIRECTION. Also vehicles as instruments play a role in the conceptualization, but not all vehicles have metaphorical attestations in the corpus: only *train* - 'train' and *bateau* - 'boat' are found during a cross-check. Finally, synsets referring to the contrary of 'move' are contained within the map of the source domain. Even the 'motor' (as a vehicle part) and its 'breakdown' (causing 'immobilization') are thus lexically and conceptually integrated in the MOTION domain derived from our corpus.

All these highlightings and hidings can be interpreted with respect to the situation of Europe before the referendum on its Constitution: Europe is made cognitively accessible as a multi-passenger vehicle in motion on a path, which has not yet arrived but is facing obstacles to its motion, possibly resulting in being stopped.

7 Conclusion and Outlook

A method for quickly finding large amounts of lexical metaphors and characterizing their source domains has been exemplified, given a target domain corpus. The method makes use of collocate exploration of a target domain keyword, in order to identify the most promising source domains. Over 1,000 manual annotations have been obtained and will be integrated into the Hamburg Metaphor Database. This outnumbers by far the results of previous studies filed within HMD, which originated under similar conditions but did not resort to a corpus manager.

Our method is different from automated work on metaphor recognition such as (Mason, 2004) and (Gedigian et al., 2006) in that it includes nouns as parts of speech. Implementing it in an automated system would require more sophisticated lexical-conceptual resources, representing information on concrete domains (possible source domains). In particular, the addition of lexical and conceptual links between verb and noun synsets is crucial for establishing a connected source domain graph.

Acknowledgements

Thanks to Patrick Hanks, Jana Klawitter, and three anonymous reviewers for their helpful comments. – This work was supported by a fellowship within the Postdoc-Programme of the German Academic Exchange Service (DAAD), granted to the second author.

References

John A. Barnden, Sheila Glasbey, Mark Lee, and Alan M. Wallington. 2002. Reasoning in metaphor understanding: The ATT-Meta approach and system. In *Proceedings of the 19th International Conference on Computational Linguistics (COLING 2002)*, pages 1188–1193, Taipei, Taiwan.

Charles J. Fillmore, Christopher R. Johnson, and Miriam R. L. Petruck. 2003. Background to FrameNet. *International Journal of Lexicography*, 16(3):235–250.

Matt Gedigian, John Bryant, Srini Narayanan, and Branimir Ciric. 2006. Catching metaphors. In *Proceedings of the 3rd Workshop on Scalable Natural Language Understanding*, pages 41–48, New York City.

George Lakoff and Mark Johnson. 1980. *Metaphors we live by*. University of Chicago Press, Chicago.

George Lakoff. 1987. *Women, fire, and dangerous things: what categories reveal about the mind*. University of Chicago Press, Chicago.

Mark Lee. 2006. Methodological issues in building a corpus of doctor-patient dialogues annotated for metaphor. In *Cognitive-linguistic approaches: What can we gain by computational treatment of data? A Theme Session at DGKL-06/GCLA-06*, pages 19–22, Munich, Germany.

Birte Lönneker and Carina Eilts. 2004. A current resource and future perspectives for enriching WordNets with metaphor information. In *Proceedings of the 2nd International Conference of the Global WordNet Association*, pages 157–162, Brno, Czech Republic.

James H. Martin. 1994. MetaBank: A knowledge-base of metaphoric language conventions. *Computational Intelligence*, 10(2):134–149.

Zachary J. Mason. 2004. CorMet: A computational, corpus-based conventional metaphor extraction system. *Computational Linguistics*, 30(1):23–44.

Pavel Rychlý and Pavel Smrž. 2004. Manatee, Bonito and Word Sketches for Czech. In *Proceedings of the Second International Conference on Corpus Linguistics*, pages 124–132, Saint-Petersburg.

Helmut Schmid. 1994. Probabilistic part-of-speech tagging using decision trees. In *International Conference on New Methods in Language Processing*, Manchester, UK.

Achim Stein and Helmut Schmid. 1995. Etiquetage morphologique de textes français avec un arbre de décisions. *Traitement automatique des langues*, 36(1-2):23–35.

Piek Vossen. 1999. EuroWordNet General Document. Version 3. Technical report, University of Amsterdam.

Hunting Elusive Metaphors Using Lexical Resources

Saisuresh Krishnakumaran*
Computer Sciences Department
University of Wisconsin-Madison
Madison, WI 53706
ksai@cs.wisc.edu

Xiaojin Zhu
Computer Sciences Department
University of Wisconsin-Madison
Madison, WI 53706
jerryzhu@cs.wisc.edu

Abstract

In this paper we propose algorithms to automatically classify sentences into metaphoric or normal usages. Our algorithms only need the WordNet and bigram counts, and does not require training. We present empirical results on a test set derived from the Master Metaphor List. We also discuss issues that make classification of metaphors a tough problem in general.

1 Introduction

Metaphor is an interesting figure of speech which expresses an analogy between two seemingly unrelated concepts. Metaphoric usages enhance the attributes of the source concept by comparing it with the attributes of the target concept. Abstractions and enormously complex situations are routinely understood via metaphors (Lakoff and Johnson, 1980). Metaphors begin their lives as Novel Poetic Creations with marked rhetoric effects whose comprehension requires special imaginative leap. As time goes by, they become part of general use and their comprehension becomes automatic and idiomatic and rhetoric effect is dulled (Nunberg, 1987). We term such metaphors whose idiomatic effects are dulled because of common usage as *dead metaphors* while metaphors with novel usages as *live metaphors*. In this paper we are interested only in identifying live metaphors.

Metaphors have interesting applications in many NLP problems like machine translation, text summarization, information retrieval and question answering. Consider the task of summarizing a parable which is a metaphoric story with a moral. The best summary of a parable is the moral. Paraphrasing a metaphoric passage like a parable is difficult without understanding the metaphoric uses. The performance of the conventional summarizing systems will be ineffective because they cannot identify such metaphoric usages. Also it is easy to create novel and interesting uses of metaphors as long as one concept is explained in terms of another concept. The performance of machine translation systems will be affected in such cases especially if they have not encountered such metaphoric uses before.

Metaphor identification in text documents is, however, complicated by issues including context sensitiveness, emergence of novel metaphoric forms, and the need for semantic knowledge about the sentences. Metaphoric appeal differs across language or people's prior exposure to such usages. In addition, as (Gibbs, 1984) points out, literal and figurative expressions are end points of a single continuum along which metaphoricity and idiomaticity are situated, thereby making clear demarcation of metaphoric and normal usages fuzzy.

We discuss many such issues that make the task of classifying sentences into metaphoric or non-metaphoric difficult. We then focuses on a subset of metaphoric usages involving the nouns in a sentence. In particular, we identify the subject-object, verb-noun and adjective-noun relationships in sentences and classify them as metaphoric or

* The first author is currently affiliated with Google Inc, Mountain View, CA.

Proceedings of the Workshop on Computational Approaches to Figurative Language, pages 13–20,
Rochester, NY, April 26, 2007.

non-metaphoric. Extensions to other metaphoric types will be part of future work. Our algorithms use the hyponym relationship in WordNet (Fellbaum, 1998), and word bigram counts, to predict the metaphors. In doing so we circumvent two issues: the absence of labeled training data, and the lack of clear features that are indicative of metaphors.

The paper is organized as follows. Section 2 presents interesting observations that were made during the initial survey, and presents examples that makes metaphor identification hard. Section 3 discusses our main techniques for identifying metaphors in text documents. Section 4 analyzes the effect of the techniques. Section 5 discusses relevant prior work in the area of metaphor processing and identification. Finally we conclude in Section 6.

2 Challenges in Metaphor Identification

In this section we present some issues that make metaphor identification hard.

2.1 Context Sensitivity

Some metaphoric usages are sensitive to the context in which they occur. For example, the following sentence can act as a normal sentence as well as a metaphoric sentence.

Men are animals.

It is a normal sentence in a biology lecture because all human beings fall under the animal kingdom. However this is a metaphoric sentence in a social conversation when it refers to animal qualities. Also the word 'Men' has two different senses in WordNet and hence it is necessary to disambiguate the senses based on the context. Sense disambiguation is beyond the scope of this paper.

2.2 Pronoun Resolution

Consider the following sentence,

This homework is a breeze. The previous one was on calculus. It was a tornado.

The techniques we discuss in this paper can classify the reference to 'breeze' as metaphoric. In order to correctly classify the reference to 'tornado' as metaphoric, however, the system needs to resolve the reference to the pronoun 'It'. Strictly speaking, this example might be solved without resolution because any of the potential antecedents render the sentence metaphoric, but in general resolution is necessary.

2.3 Word Usages

Consider the following two sentences,

He is a Gandhi. vs. *He is Gandhi.*

The first sentence is a metaphor which attributes the qualities of Gandhi to the actor, while the second sentence is a normal one. Here the article 'a' distinguishes the first sentence from the second. Similarly, in the following example, the phrase 'among men' helps in making the second usage metaphoric.

He is a king. vs. *He is a king among men.*

A comprehensive list of such uses are not known and incorporating all such grammatical features would make the system quite complex.

2.4 Parser Issues

The techniques that we propose work on the parsed sentences. Hence the accuracy of our technique is highly dependent on the accuracy of the parser.

2.5 Metaphoric Usages in WordNet

Some metaphoric senses of nouns are already part of the WordNet.

He is a wolf.

The metaphoric sense of 'wolf' is directly mentioned in the WordNet. We call such usages as 'dead metaphors' because they are so common and are already part of the lexicon. In this paper we are interested in identifying only novel usages of metaphors.

3 Noun-Form Metaphors

We restrict ourselves to metaphoric usages involving nouns. In particular, we study the effect of verbs and adjectives on the nouns in a sentence. We categorize the verb-noun relationship in sentences as Type I and Type II based on the verb. We call the adjective-noun relationship as Type III, see Table 1.

For Type I, the verb is one of the 'be' form verbs like 'is', 'are', 'am', 'was', etc. An example of Type I form metaphor is

Table 1: Terminology

Sentence Type	Relationship
Type I	Subject IS-A Object
Type II	Verb acting on Noun (verb not 'be')
Type III	Adjective acting on Noun

He is a brave lion.

An example of Type II form metaphor is

He planted good ideas in their minds.

An example for Type III form metaphor is

He has a fertile imagination.

We use two different approaches for Type I vs. Types II, III. In Type I form we are interested in the relationship between the subject and the object. We use a hyponym heuristic. In Types II and III, we are interested in the subject-verb, verb-object, or adjective-noun relations. We use hyponym together with word co-occurrence information, in this case bigrams from the Web 1T corpus (Brants and Franz, 2006). Sections 3.1 and 3.2 discuss the two algorithms, respectively. We use a parser (Klein and Manning, 2003) to obtain the relationships between nouns, verbs and adjectives in a sentence.

3.1 Identifying Type I metaphors

We identify the WordNet hyponym relationship (or the lack thereof) between the subject and the object in a Type I sentence. We classify the sentence as metaphoric, if the subject and object does not have a hyponym relation. A hyponym relation exists between a pair of words if and only if one word is a subclass of another word. We motivate this idea using some examples. Let us consider a normal sentence with a subject-object relationship governed by a 'be' form verb, 'is'.

A lion is a wild animal.

The subject-verb-object relationship of this normal sentence is shown in Figure 1.

The subject and the object in the above example is governed by 'IS-A' relationship. Thus, Lion 'IS-A' type of animal. The 'IS-A' relationship is captured

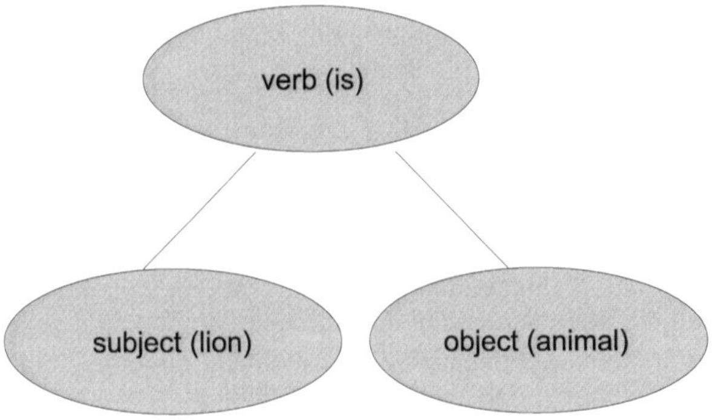

Figure 1: The Subject-Verb-Object relationship for 'A lion is a wild animal.'

as the 'hyponym' relationship in WordNet, where 'Lion' is the hyponym of 'animal'. Consider another example,

He is a scientist.

Here the object 'scientist' is the occupation of the subject 'He', which we change to 'person'. 'Scientist' is a hyponym of 'person' in WordNet. The above two examples show that we expect a subject-object hyponym relation for normal Type I relations. On the other hand, consider a metaphoric example in Type I form,

All the world's a stage.
- William Shakespeare

The subject-verb-object relationship is represented by Figure 2.

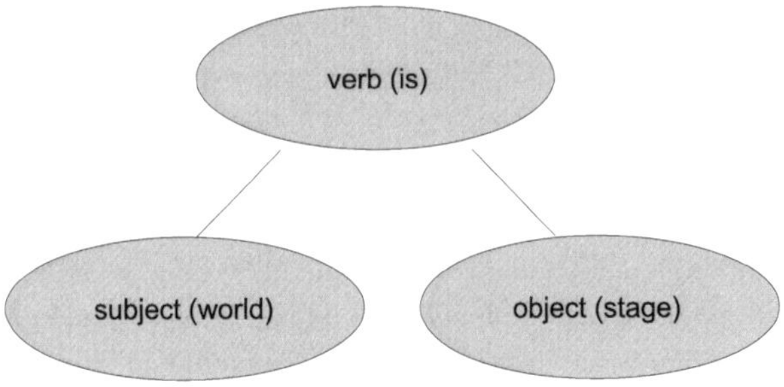

Figure 2: The Subject-Verb-Object relationship for 'All the world is a stage.'

There is a subject-object relation between 'World' and 'Stage', but they do not hold a hyponym relation in WordNet. This is an important observation which we use in classifying relationships of this form. Consider another example with complex sentences,

> *Men are April when they woo, December when they wed. Maids are May when they are maids, but the sky changes when they are wives.*
> *-Shakespeare's 'As You Like It'.*

In this case, there are two explicit subject-object relations, namely Men-April and Maids-May. The WordNet hyponym relation does not exist between either pair.

From the examples considered above, it is seems that when a hyponym relation exists between the subject and the object, the relationship is normal, and metaphoric otherwise. The effectiveness of this approach is analyzed in detail in Section 4. The pseudo code for classifying Type I relations is given below:

1. Parse the sentences and get all R $\leftarrow$ {subject, be, object} relations in those sentences.

2. for each relation $\mathrm{R}_{sub,obj}$

   if Hyponym(sub,obj) = true

   then $\mathrm{R}_{sub,obj}$ is normal usage

   else $\mathrm{R}_{sub,obj}$ is a metaphoric relation

3. All sentences with at least one metaphoric relation is classified as metaphoric.

3.2 Identifying Type II and Type III metaphors

We use a two dimensional V/A-N co-occurrence matrix, in addition to WordNet, for detecting Type II and Type III metaphors. V/A-N matrix stands for Verb/Adjective-Noun matrix, which is a two dimensional matrix with verbs or adjectives along one dimension, and nouns along the other. The entries are co-occurrence frequency of the word pair, from which we may estimate the conditional probability $p(w_n|w)$ for a noun w_n and a verb or adjective w. Ideally the matrix should be constructed from a parsed corpus, so that we can identify V/A-N pairs from their syntactic roles. However parsing a large corpus would be prohibitively expensive. As a practical approximation, we use bigram counts from the Web 1T corpus (Brants and Franz, 2006). Web 1T corpus consists of English word n-grams (up to 5-grams) generated from approximately 1 trillion word tokens of text from public Web pages. In this paper we use the bigram data in which a noun follows either a verb or an adjective. We note that this approximation thus misses, for example, the pair (plant, idea) in phrases like 'plant an idea'. Nonetheless, the hope is that the corpus makes it up by sheer size.

3.2.1 Type II metaphors

We discuss the metaphoric relationship between a verb-noun pair (w_v, w_n). The idea is that if neither w_n nor its hyponyms or hypernyms co-occur frequently with w_v, then the pair is a novel usage, and we classify the pair as metaphoric. To this end, we estimate the conditional probability $p(w_h|w_v) = \text{count}(w_v, w_h)/\text{count}(w_v)$ from the V/A-N matrix, where w_h is w_n itself, or one of its hyponyms / hypernyms. If at least one of these w_h has high enough conditional probability as determined by a threshold, we classify it as normal usage, and metaphoric otherwise. Consider the following example

> *He planted good ideas in their minds.*

The verb 'planted' acts on the noun 'ideas' and makes the sentence metaphoric. In our corpus the objects that occur more frequently with the verb 'planted' are 'trees', 'bomb' and 'wheat', etc. Neither the noun 'ideas' nor its hyponyms / hypernyms occurs frequently enough with 'planted'. Hence we predict this verb-object relationship as metaphoric. The pseudo code for classifying Type II metaphors is given below:

1. Parse the sentences and obtain all R $\leftarrow$ {verb, noun} relations in those sentences.

2. for each relation $\mathrm{R}_{verb,noun}$

   Sort all nouns w in the vocabulary by decreasing $p(w|verb)$. Take the smallest set of top k nouns whose conditional probability sum $\geq$ threshold T.

   if $\exists w_h$ such that w_h is related to $noun$ by the hyponym relation in WordNet, and $w_h \in$ top k words above,

   then $\mathrm{R}_{verb,noun}$ is normal usage

   else $\mathrm{R}_{verb,noun}$ is a Type II metaphoric relation

3. All sentences with at least one metaphoric relationship is classified as a metaphor.

3.2.2 Type III metaphors

The technique for detecting the Type III metaphors is the same as the technique for detecting the Type II metaphors except that it operates on different relationship. Here we compare the Adjective-Noun relationship instead of the Verb-Noun relationship. For example,

He has a fertile imagination.

Here the adjective 'fertile' acts on the noun 'imagination' to make it metaphoric. The nouns that occur frequently with the 'fertile' in our corpus are 'soil', 'land', 'territory', and 'plains', etc. Comparison of the WordNet hierarchies of the noun 'imagination' with each of these nouns will show that there does not exist any hyponym relation between 'imagination' and any of these nouns. Hence we classify them as metaphors. As another example,

TV is an idiot box.

The adjective 'idiot' qualifies nouns related to people such as 'boy', 'man', etc. that are unrelated to the noun 'box'. Thus we classify it as a Type III metaphor.

4 Experimental Results

We experimented with the Berkeley Master Metaphor List (Lakoff and Johnson, 1980) to compute the performance of our techniques. The Berkeley Master Metaphor List is a collection of nearly 1728 unique sentences and phrases. We corrected some typos and spelling errors in the Master list and expanded phrases to complete sentences. The list has many metaphoric uses which has become very common usages in today's standards, and thus no longer have any rhetoric effects. Therefore, we manually label the sentences in the Master List into 789 'live metaphors' and the remaining ones 'dead metaphors' as the ground truth[1].

Table 2 shows the initial performance of the Type I algorithm. There are 129 sentences in the Master List that contain subject-be-object form. Our algorithm has a precision of 70% and a recall of 61% with respect to the live/dead labels. Note that although the accuracy is 58%, the algorithm is better than a random classification in terms of precision and recall. One thing to note is that our negative examples are (subjectively labeled) dead metaphors. We thus expect the task to be harder than with random non-metaphoric sentences. Another point to note here is that the live/dead labels are on sentences and not on particular phrases with type I relations. A sentence can contain more than one phrases with various types. Therefore this result does not give a complete picture of our algorithm.

Table 2: Type I Performance

	Predicted as Metaphoric	Predicted as Normal
Annotated as live	50	32
Annotated as dead	22	25

A few interesting metaphors detected by our algorithm are as follows:

Lawyers are real sharks.
Smog pollution is an environmental malaise.

Some false negatives are due to phrases qualifying the object of the sentence as in the following example,

He is a budding artist.

There is a Type I relation in this sentence because the subject 'He' and the object 'artist' are related by the 'be' form verb 'is'. In this case, the Type I algorithm compares the hyponyms relation between 'person' and 'artist' and declares it as a normal sentence. However the adjective 'budding' adds Type III figurative meaning to this sentence. Therefore although the Type I relation is normal, there are other features in the sentences that make it metaphoric. We observed that most of false negatives that are wrongly classified because of the above reason have pronoun subject like 'he', 'she' etc.

Another major source of issue is the occurrences of pronoun 'it' which is hard to resolve. We replaced it by 'entity', which is the root of WordNet, when

[1]Our processed and labeled dataset is available at `http://www.cs.wisc.edu/~ksai/publications/2007/HLT_NAACL_metaphors/metaphors.html`

comparing the hyponyms. 'Entity' matches the hyponym relation with any other noun and hence all these sentences with 'it' as the subject are classified as normal sentences.

Table 3: Type I Performance for sentences with non-pronoun subject

	Predicted as Metaphoric	Predicted as Normal
Annotated as live	40	1
Annotated as dead	19	4

Table 3 shows the performance of our Type I algorithm for sentences with non-pronoun subjects. It clearly shows that the performance in Table 2 is affected by sentences with pronoun subjects as explained in the earlier paragraphs.

In some cases, prepositional phrases affects the performance of our algorithm. Consider the following example,

He is the child of evil.

Here the phrase 'child of evil' is metaphoric. But the parser identifies a subject-be-object relationship between 'He' and 'child' and our algorithm compares the hyponym relation between 'person' and 'child' and declares it as a normal sentence.

Our current algorithm does not deal with cases like the following example

The customer is a scientist. vs. The customer is king.

Since there is no direct hyponym relation between scientist/king with customer we declare both these sentences as metaphors although only the latter is.

Unlike the algorithm for Type I, there is a threshold T to be set for Type II and III algorithm. By changing T, we are able to plot a precision recall curve. Figure 3 and figure 4 show the precision recall graph for Type II and Type III relations respectively. Figure 5 shows the overall precision recall graph for all three types put together.

False positives in Type II and Type III were due to very general verbs and adjectives. These verbs and adjectives can occur with a large number of nouns, and tend to produce low conditional probabilities even for normal nouns. Thereby they are often mistakenly classified as metaphoric relations. We expect the performance to improve if these general verbs and adjectives are handled properly. Some general verbs include 'gave', 'made', 'has', etc., and similarity general adjectives include 'new', 'good', 'many', 'more', etc. The plot for Type III is more random.

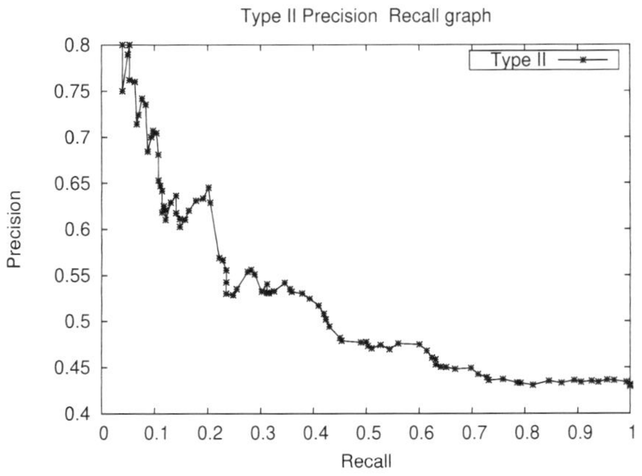

Figure 3: Precision Recall curve for Type II relations.

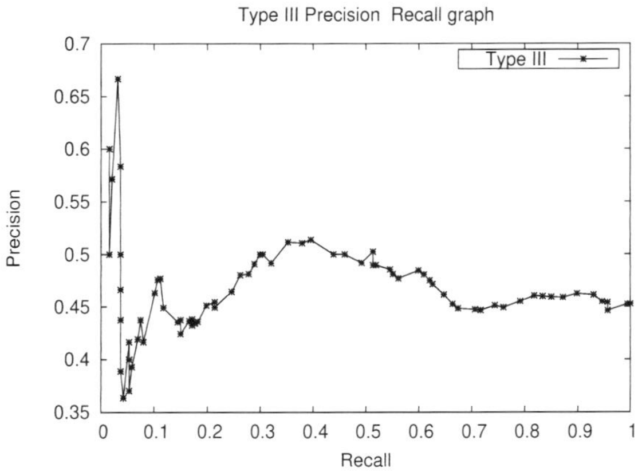

Figure 4: Precision Recall curve for Type III relations.

Most errors can be attributed to some of the following reasons:

- As mentioned in the challenges section, the parser is not very accurate. For example,

  They battled each other over the chess board every week.

  Here the parser identifies the verb-object relation as (battled , week), which is not correct.

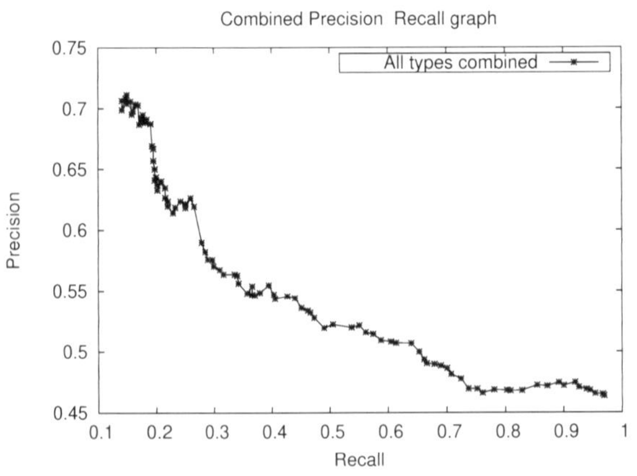

Figure 5: Overall Precision Recall curve for all three types combined.

- Pronoun resolution: As discussed earlier, the pronoun 'it' is not resolved and hence they introduce additional source of errors.
- Manual annotations could be wrong. In our experiment we have used only two annotators, but having more would have increased the confidence in the labels.
- Many of the verb-noun forms are most naturally captured by trigrams instead of bigram. For example, (developed , attachment) most likely occurs in a corpus as 'developed an attachment' or 'developed the attachment'. Our bigram approach can fail here.
- Sense disambiguation: We don't disambiguate senses while comparing the WordNet relations. This increases our false negatives.
- Also as mentioned earlier, the labels are on sentences and not on the typed relationships. Therefore even though a sentence has one or more of the noun form types, those may be normal relationships while the whole sentence may be metaphoric because of other types. Note, however, that some of these mismatches are corrected for the 'All types combined' result.

5 Related Work

There has been a long history of research in metaphors. We briefly review some of them here. One thing that sets our work apart is that most previous literatures in this area tend to give little empirical evaluation of their approaches. In contrast, in this study we provide detailed analysis of the effectiveness of our approaches.

(Fass and Wilks, 1983) proposes the use of preference semantics for metaphor recognition. Techniques for automatically detecting selections preferences have been discussed in (McCarthy and Carrol, 2003) and (Resnik, 1997). Type II and Type III approaches discussed in this paper uses both these ideas for detecting live metaphors. Fass (Fass, 1991) uses selectional preference violation technique to detect metaphors. However they rely on hand-coded declarative knowledge bases. Our technique depends only on WordNet and we use selection preference violation based on the knowledge learned from the bigram frequencies on the Web.

Markert and Nissim (Markert and Nissim, 2002) presents a supervised classification algorithm for resolving metonymy. Metonymy is a closely related figure of speech to metaphors where a word is substituted by another with which it is associated. Example,

A pen is mightier than a sword.

Here sword is a metonymy for war and pen is a metonymy for articles. They use collocation, co-occurrence and grammatical features in their classification algorithm.

MetaBank (Martin, 1994) is a large knowledge base of metaphors empirically collected. The detection technique compares new sentences with this knowledge base. The accuracy is dependent on the correctness of the knowledge base and we expect that some of these metaphors would be dead in the present context. The techniques we discuss in this work will drastically reduce the need for manually constructing such a large collection.

Goatly (Goatly, 1997) proposes using analogy markers such as 'like', 'such as', 'illustrated by' and lexical markers like 'literally', 'illustrating', 'metaphorically' etc. These would be useful for identifying simile and explicit metaphoric relations but not metaphors where the relation between the target concept and the source concept is not explicit.

The CorMet system (Mason, 2004) dynamically mines domain specific corpora to find less frequent usages and identifies conceptual metaphors. However the system is limited to extracting only selectional preferences of verbs. Verbal selectional preference is the verb's preference for the type of argument it takes.

Dolan (Dolan, 1995) uses the path and path length between words in the knowledge base derived from lexical resources for interpreting the interrelationship between the component parts of a metaphor. The effectiveness of this technique relies on whether the metaphoric sense is encoded in the dictionaries. This approach however will not be effective for novel metaphoric usages that are not encoded in dictionaries.

6 Conclusion

In this paper we show that we can use the hyponym relation in WordNet and word co-occurrence information for detecting metaphoric uses in subject-object, verb-noun and adjective-noun relationships. According to (Cameron and Deignan, 2006), non literal expressions with relatively fixed forms and highly specific semantics are over-represented in the metaphor literature in comparison to corpora occurrences. Therefore as part of future work we would be studying the effect of our algorithms for naturally occurring text. We are also interested in increasing the confidence of the labels using more and diverse annotators and see how the techniques perform. The study can then be extended to incorporate the role of prepositions in metaphoric uses.

7 Acknowledgment

We would like to thank our anonymous reviewers for their constructive suggestions that helped improve this paper. We would also like to thank Mr. Krishna Kumaran Damodaran for annotating the Master Metaphor List.

References

Thorsten Brants and Alex Franz. 2006. *Web 1T 5-gram Version 1*. Linguistic Data Consortium, Philadelphia.

Lynne Cameron and Alice Deignan. 2006. The emergence of metaphor in discourse. *Applied Linguistics*, 27(4):671–690.

William B. Dolan. 1995. Metaphor as an emergent property of machine-readable dictionaries. *AAAI 1995 Spring Symposium*, 95(1):27–32.

Dan Fass and Yorick Wilks. 1983. Preference semantics, ill-formedness, and metaphor. *American Journal of Computational Linguistics*, 9(3):178–187.

Dan Fass. 1991. Met: A method for discriminating metonymy and metaphor by computer. *Computational Linguistics*, 17(1):49–90.

Christiane Fellbaum, editor. 1998. *WordNet: An Electronic Lexical Database*. MIT Press, Cambridge, MA.

Raymond Gibbs. 1984. Literal meaning and psychological theory. *Cognitive Science*, 8:275–304.

Andrew Goatly. 1997. *The Language of Metaphors*. Routledge,London.

Dan Klein and Christopher D. Manning. 2003. Accurate unlexicalized parsing. In *Proceedings of the 41st Meeting of the Association for Computational Linguistics*.

George Lakoff and Mark Johnson. 1980. *Metaphors We Live By*. University of Chicago Press, Chicago, Illinois.

Katja Markert and Malvina Nissim. 2002. Metonymy resolution as a classifi cation task. In *Proceedings of ACL-02 conference on Empirical Methods in Natural Language Processing*, pages 204–213.

James H. Martin. 1994. Metabank: a knowledge-base of metaphoric language conventions. *Computational Intelligence*, 10(2):134–149.

Zachary J. Mason. 2004. Cormet: A computational, corpus-based conventional metaphor extraction system. *Computational Linguistics*, 30(1):23–44.

Diana McCarthy and John Carrol. 2003. Disambiguating nouns, verbs and adjectives using automatically acquired selectional preferences. *Computational Linguistics*, 29(4):639–654.

Geoffrey Nunberg. 1987. Poetic and prosaic metaphors. In *Proceedings of the 1987 workshop on Theoretical issues in natural language processing*, pages 198–201.

Philip Resnik. 1997. Selectional preferences and word sense disambiguation. In *Proceedings of ACL Siglex Workshop on Tagging Text with Lexical Semantics, Why, What and How?, Washington, D.C.*, pages 52–57.

Active Learning for the Identification of Nonliteral Language *

Julia Birke and Anoop Sarkar
School of Computing Science, Simon Fraser University
Burnaby, BC, V5A 1S6, Canada
jbirke@alumni.sfu.ca, anoop@cs.sfu.ca

Abstract

In this paper we present an active learning approach used to create an annotated corpus of literal and nonliteral usages of verbs. The model uses nearly unsupervised word-sense disambiguation and clustering techniques. We report on experiments in which a human expert is asked to correct system predictions in different stages of learning: (i) after the last iteration when the clustering step has converged, or (ii) during each iteration of the clustering algorithm. The model obtains an f-score of 53.8% on a dataset in which literal/nonliteral usages of 25 verbs were annotated by human experts. In comparison, the same model augmented with active learning obtains 64.91%. We also measure the *number* of examples required when model confidence is used to select examples for human correction as compared to random selection. The results of this active learning system have been compiled into a freely available annotated corpus of literal/nonliteral usage of verbs in context.

1 Introduction

In this paper, we propose a largely automated method for creating an annotated corpus of literal vs. nonliteral usages of verbs. For example, given the verb "pour", we would expect our method to identify the sentence "Custom demands that cognac be *poured* from a freshly opened bottle" as literal, and the sentence "Salsa and rap music *pour* out of the windows" as nonliteral, which, indeed, it does.

We reduce the problem of nonliteral language recognition to one of word-sense disambiguation (WSD) by redefining *literal* and *nonliteral* as two different senses of the same word, and we adapt an existing similarity-based word-sense disambiguation method to the task of separating usages of verbs into literal and nonliteral clusters. Note that treating this task as similar to WSD only means that we use features from the local context around the verb to identify it as either literal or non-literal. It does not mean that we can use a classifier trained on WSD annotated corpora to solve this issue, or use any existing WSD classification technique that relies on supervised learning. We do not have any annotated data to train such a classifier, and indeed our work is focused on building such a dataset. Indeed our work aims to first discover reliable seed data and then bootstrap a literal/nonliteral identification model. Also, we cannot use any semi-supervised learning algorithm for WSD which relies on reliably annotated seed data since we do not possess any reliably labeled data (except for our test data set). However we do exploit a noisy source of seed data in a nearly unsupervised approach augmented with active learning. Noisy data containing example sentences of literal and nonliteral usage of verbs is used in our model to cluster a particular instance of a verb into one class or the other. This paper focuses on the use of active learning using this model. We suggest that this approach produces a large saving of effort compared to creating such an annotated corpus manually.

An active learning approach to machine learning is one in which the learner has the ability to influence the selection of at least a portion of its training data. In our approach, a clustering algorithm for literal/nonliteral recognition tries to annotate the examples that it can, while in each iteration it sends a small set of examples to a human expert to annotate, which in turn provides additional benefit to the bootstrapping process. Our active learn-

*This research was partially supported by NSERC, Canada (RGPIN: 264905). We would like to thank Bill Dolan, Fred Popowich, Dan Fass, Katja Markert, Yudong Liu, and the anonymous reviewers for their comments.

Proceedings of the Workshop on Computational Approaches to Figurative Language, pages 21–28,
Rochester, NY, April 26, 2007. ©2007 Association for Computational Linguistics

ing method is similar to the Uncertainty Sampling algorithm of (Lewis & Gale, 1994) but in our case interacts with iterative clustering. As we shall see, some of the crucial criticisms leveled against uncertainty sampling and in favor of Committee-based sampling (Engelson & Dagan, 1996) do not apply in our case, although the latter may still be more accurate in our task.

2 Literal vs. Nonliteral Identification

For the purposes of this paper we will take the simplified view that *literal* is anything that falls within accepted selectional restrictions ("he was forced to eat his spinach" vs. "he was forced to eat his words") or our knowledge of the world ("the sponge absorbed the water" vs. "the company absorbed the loss"). *Nonliteral* is then anything that is "not literal", including most tropes, such as metaphors, idioms, as well as phrasal verbs and other anomalous expressions that cannot really be seen as *literal*. We aim to automatically discover the contrast between the standard set of selectional restrictions for the literal usage of verbs and the non-standard set which we assume will identify the nonliteral usage.

Our identification model for literal vs. nonliteral usage of verbs is described in detail in a previous publication (Birke & Sarkar, 2006). Here we provide a brief description of the model so that the use of this model in our proposed active learning approach can be explained.

Since we are attempting to reduce the problem of literal/nonliteral recognition to one of word-sense disambiguation, we use an existing similarity-based word-sense disambiguation algorithm developed by (Karov & Edelman, 1998), henceforth KE. The KE algorithm is based on the principle of attraction: similarities are calculated between sentences containing the word we wish to disambiguate (the *target word*) and collections of seed sentences (*feedback sets*). It requires a *target set* – the set of sentences containing the verbs to be classified into literal or nonliteral – and the seed sets: the *literal feedback set* and the *nonliteral feedback set*. A target set sentence is considered to be attracted to the feedback set containing the sentence to which it shows the highest similarity. Two sentences are similar if they contain similar words and two words are similar if they are contained in similar sentences. The resulting *transitive similarity* allows us to defeat the *knowledge acquisition bottleneck* – i.e. the low likelihood of finding all possible usages of a word in a single corpus. Note that the KE algorithm concentrates on similarities in the way sentences use the target literal or nonliteral word, not on similarities in the meanings of the sentences themselves.

Algorithms 1 and 2 summarize our approach. Note that $p(w, s)$ is the unigram probability of word w in sentence s, normalized by the total number of words in s. We omit some details about the algorithm here which do not affect our discussion about active learning. These details are provided in a previous publication (Birke & Sarkar, 2006).

As explained before, our model requires a target set and two seed sets: the literal feedback set and the nonliteral feedback set. We do not explain the details of how these feedback sets were constructed in this paper, however, it is important to note that the feedback sets themselves are noisy and not carefully vetted by human experts. The literal feedback set was built from WSJ newswire text, and for the nonliteral feedback set, we use expressions from various datasets such as the Wayne Magnuson English Idioms Sayings & Slang and George Lakoff's Conceptual Metaphor List, as well as example sentences from these sources. These datasets provide lists of verbs that may be used in a nonliteral usage, but we cannot explicitly provide only those sentences that contain nonliteral use of that verb in the nonliteral feedback set. In particular, knowing that an expression *can* be used nonliterally does not mean that you can tell when it *is* being used nonliterally. In fact even the literal feedback set has noise from nonliteral uses of verbs in the news articles. To deal with this issue (Birke & Sarkar, 2006) provides automatic methods to clean up the feedback sets during the clustering algorithm. Note that the feedback sets are not cleaned up by human experts, however the test data is carefully annotated by human experts (details about inter-annotator agreement on the test set are provided below). The test set is not large enough to be split up into a training and test set that can support learning using a supervised learning method.

The sentences in the target set and feedback sets were augmented with some shallow syntactic information such as part of speech tags provided

Algorithm 1 *KE-train*: (Karov & Edelman, 1998) algorithm adapted to literal/nonliteral identification

Require: $\mathcal{S}$: the set of sentences containing the *target word* (each sentence is classified as literal/nonliteral)
Require: $\mathcal{L}$: the set of literal seed sentences
Require: $\mathcal{N}$: the set of nonliteral seed sentences
Require: $\mathcal{W}$: the set of words/features, $w \in s$ means w is in sentence s, $s \ni w$ means s contains w
Require: ϵ: threshold that determines the stopping condition

$\textit{w-sim}_0(w_x, w_y) := 1$ *if* $w_x = w_y$, 0 *otherwise*
$\textit{s-sim}_0^I(s_x, s_y) := 1$, for all $s_x, s_y \in \mathcal{S} \times \mathcal{S}$ where $s_x = s_y$, 0 otherwise
$i := 0$
while (**true**) **do**
  $\textit{s-sim}_{i+1}^L(s_x, s_y) := \sum_{w_x \in s_x} p(w_x, s_x) \max_{w_y \in s_y} \textit{w-sim}_i(w_x, w_y)$, for all $s_x, s_y \in \mathcal{S} \times \mathcal{L}$
  $\textit{s-sim}_{i+1}^N(s_x, s_y) := \sum_{w_x \in s_x} p(w_x, s_x) \max_{w_y \in s_y} \textit{w-sim}_i(w_x, w_y)$, for all $s_x, s_y \in \mathcal{S} \times \mathcal{N}$
  for $w_x, w_y \in \mathcal{W} \times \mathcal{W}$ **do**
    $$\textit{w-sim}_{i+1}(w_x, w_y) := \begin{cases} i = 0 & \sum_{s_x \ni w_x} p(w_x, s_x) \max_{s_y \ni w_y} \textit{s-sim}_i^I(s_x, s_y) \\ \text{else} & \sum_{s_x \ni w_x} p(w_x, s_x) \max_{s_y \ni w_y} \{\textit{s-sim}_i^L(s_x, s_y), \textit{s-sim}_i^N(s_x, s_y)\} \end{cases}$$
  end for
  if $\forall w_x, \max_{w_y} \{\textit{w-sim}_{i+1}(w_x, w_y) - \textit{w-sim}_i(w_x, w_y)\} \leq \epsilon$ **then**
    break # algorithm converges in $\frac{1}{\epsilon}$ steps.
  end if
  $i := i + 1$
end while

by a statistical tagger (Ratnaparkhi, 1996) and SuperTags (Bangalore & Joshi, 1999).

This model was evaluated on 25 target verbs:

> absorb, assault, die, drag, drown, escape, examine, fill, fix, flow, grab, grasp, kick, knock, lend, miss, pass, rest, ride, roll, smooth, step, stick, strike, touch

The verbs were carefully chosen to have varying token frequencies (we do not simply learn on frequently occurring verbs). As a result, the target sets contain from 1 to 115 manually annotated sentences for each verb to enable us to measure accuracy. The annotations were not provided to the learning algorithm: they were only used to evaluate the test data performance. The first round of annotations was done by the first annotator. The second annotator was given no instructions besides a few examples of literal and nonliteral usage (not covering all target verbs). The authors of this paper were the annotators. Our inter-annotator agreement on the annotations used as test data in the experiments in this paper is quite high. κ (Cohen) *and* κ (S&C) on a random sample of 200 annotated examples annotated by two different annotators was found to be 0.77. As per ((Di Eugenio & Glass, 2004), cf. refs therein), the standard assessment for κ values is that tentative conclusions on agreement exists when $.67 \leq \kappa < .8$, and a definite conclusion on agreement exists when $\kappa \geq .8$.

In the case of a larger scale annotation effort, having the person leading the effort provide one or two examples of literal and nonliteral usages for each target verb to each annotator would almost certainly improve inter-annotator agreement.

The algorithms were evaluated based on how accurately they clustered the hand-annotated sentences. Sentences that were attracted to neither cluster or were equally attracted to both were put in the opposite set from their label, making a failure to cluster a sentence an incorrect clustering.

Evaluation results were recorded as *recall*, *precision*, and *f-score* values. *Literal recall* is defined as *(correct literals in literal cluster / total correct literals)*. *Literal precision* is defined as *(correct literals in literal cluster / size of literal cluster)*. If there are no literals, *literal recall* is 100%; *literal precision* is 100% if there are no nonliterals in the literal cluster and 0% otherwise. The *f-score* is defined as *(2 ·*

Algorithm 2 *KE-test*: classifying literal/nonliteral

1: For any sentence $s_x \in \mathcal{S}$
2: **if** $\max_{s_y} s\text{-}sim^L(s_x, s_y) > \max_{s_y} s\text{-}sim^N(s_x, s_y)$ **then**
3: tag s_x as literal
4: **else**
5: tag s_x as nonliteral
6: **end if**

precision · recall) / (precision + recall). Nonliteral precision and recall are defined similarly. Average precision is the average of literal and nonliteral precision; similarly for average recall. For overall performance, we take the f-score of average precision and average recall.

We calculated two baselines for each word. The first was a simple majority-rules baseline (assign each word to the sense which is dominant which is always literal in our dataset). Due to the imbalance of literal and nonliteral examples, this baseline ranges from 60.9% to 66.7% for different verbs with an average of 63.6%. Keep in mind though that using this baseline, the f-score for the nonliteral set will always be 0% – which is the problem we are trying to solve in this work. We calculated a second baseline using a simple attraction algorithm. Each sentence in the target set is attracted to the feedback set with which it has the most words in common. For the baseline and for our own model, sentences attracted to neither, or equally to both sets are put in the opposite cluster to which they belong. This second baseline obtains a f-score of 29.36% while the weakly supervised model without active learning obtains an f-score of 53.8%. Results for each verb are shown in Figure 1.

3 Active Learning

The model described thus far is weakly supervised. The main proposal in this paper is to push the results further by adding in an active learning component, which puts the model described in Section 2 in the position of helping a human expert with the literal/nonliteral clustering task. The two main points to consider are: *what* to send to the human annotator, and *when* to send it.

We always send sentences from the undecided cluster – i.e. those sentences where attraction to either feedback set, or the absolute difference of the two attractions, falls below a given threshold. The number of sentences falling under this threshold varies considerably from word to word, so we additionally impose a predetermined cap on the number of sentences that can ultimately be sent to the human. Based on an experiment on a held-out set separate from our target set of sentences, sending a maximum of 30% of the original set was determined to be optimal in terms of eventual accuracy obtained. We impose an order on the candidate sentences using similarity values. This allows the original sentences with the least similarity to either feedback set to be sent to the human first. Further, we alternate positive similarity (or absolute difference) values and values of zero. Note that sending examples that score zero to the human may not help attract new sentences to either of the feedback sets (since scoring zero means that the sentence was not attracted to any of the sentences). However, human help may be the only chance these sentences have to be clustered at all.

After the human provides an identification for a particular example we move the sentence not only into the correct cluster, but also into the corresponding feedback set so that other sentences might be attracted to this certifiably correctly classified sentence.

The second question is when to send the sentences to the human. We can send all the examples after the first iteration, after some intermediate iteration, distributed across iterations, or at the end. Sending everything after the first iteration is best for counteracting false attractions before they become entrenched and for allowing future iterations to learn from the human decisions. Risks include sending sentences to the human before our model has had a chance to make potentially correct decision about them, counteracting any saving of effort. (Karov & Edelman, 1998) state that the results are not likely to change much after the third iteration and we have confirmed this independently: similarity values continue to change until convergence, but cluster allegiance tends not to. Sending everything to the human after the third iteration could therefore entail some of the damage control of sending everything after the first iteration while giving the model a chance to do its best. Another possibility is to send the sentences in small doses in order to gain some bootstrapping benefit at each iteration i.e. the certainty measures will improve with each bit of human input, so at each iteration more appropriate sentences will be sent to the human. Ideally, this would produce a compounding of benefits. On the other hand, it could produce a compounding of risks. A final possibility is to wait until the last iteration in the hope that our model has correctly clustered everything else and those correctly labeled examples do not need to be examined by the human. This immediately destroys any bootstrapping possibilities for the current run, although it still provides benefits for iterative augmentation runs (see Section 4).

A summary of our results in shown in Figure 1. The last column in the graph shows the average across all the target verbs. We now discuss the various active learning experiments we performed using our model and a human expert annotator.

3.1 Experiment 1

Experiments were performed to determine the best time to send up to 30% of the sentences to the human annotator. Sending everything after the first iteration produced an average accuracy of 66.8%; sending everything after the third iteration, 65.2%; sending a small amount at each iteration, 60.8%; sending everything after the last iteration, 64.9%. Going just by the average accuracy, the first iteration option seems optimal. However, several of the individual word results fell catastrophically below the baseline, mainly due to original sentences having been moved into a feedback set too early, causing false attraction. This risk was compounded in the distributed case, as predicted. The third iteration option gave slightly better results (0.3%) than the last iteration option, but since the difference was minor, we opted for the stability of sending everything after the last iteration. These results show an improvement of 11.1% over the model from Section 2. Individual results for each verb are given in Figure 1.

3.2 Experiment 2

In a second experiment, rather than letting our model select the sentences to send to the human, we selected them randomly. We found no significant difference in the results. For the random model to outperform the non-random one it would have to select only sentences that our model would have clustered incorrectly; to do worse it would have to select only sentences that our model could have handled on its own. The likelihood of the random choices coming exclusively from these two sets is low.

3.3 Experiment 3

Our third experiment considers the effort-savings of using our literal/nonliteral identification model. The main question must be whether the 11.1% accuracy gain of active learning is worth the effort the human must contribute. In our experiments, the human annotator is given at most 30% of the sentences to classify manually. It is expected that the human will classify these correctly and any additional accuracy gain is contributed by the model. Without semi-supervised learning, we might expect that if the human were to manually classify 30% of the sentences chosen at random, he would have 30% of the sentences classified correctly. However, in order to be able to compare the human-only scenario to the active learning scenario, we must find what the average f-score of the manual process is. The f-score depends on the distribution of literal and nonliteral sentences in the original set. For example, in a set of 100 sentences, if there are exactly 50 of each, and of the 30 chosen for manual annotation, half come from the literal set and half come from the nonliteral set, the f-score will be exactly 30%. We could compare our performance to this, but that would be unfair to the manual process since the sets on which we did our evaluation were by no means balanced. We base a hypothetical scenario on the heavy imbalance often seen in our evaluation sets, and suggest a situation where 96 of our 100 sentences are literal and only 4 are nonliteral. If it were to happen that all 4 of the nonliteral sentences were sent to the human, we would get a very high f-score, due to a perfect recall score for the nonliteral cluster and a perfect precision score for the literal cluster. If none of the four nonliteral sentences were sent to the human, the scores for the nonliteral cluster would be disastrous. This situation is purely hypothetical, but should account for the fact that 30 out of 100 sentences annotated by a human will not necessarily result in an average f-score of 30%: in fact, averaging the results of the three sitatuations described above results

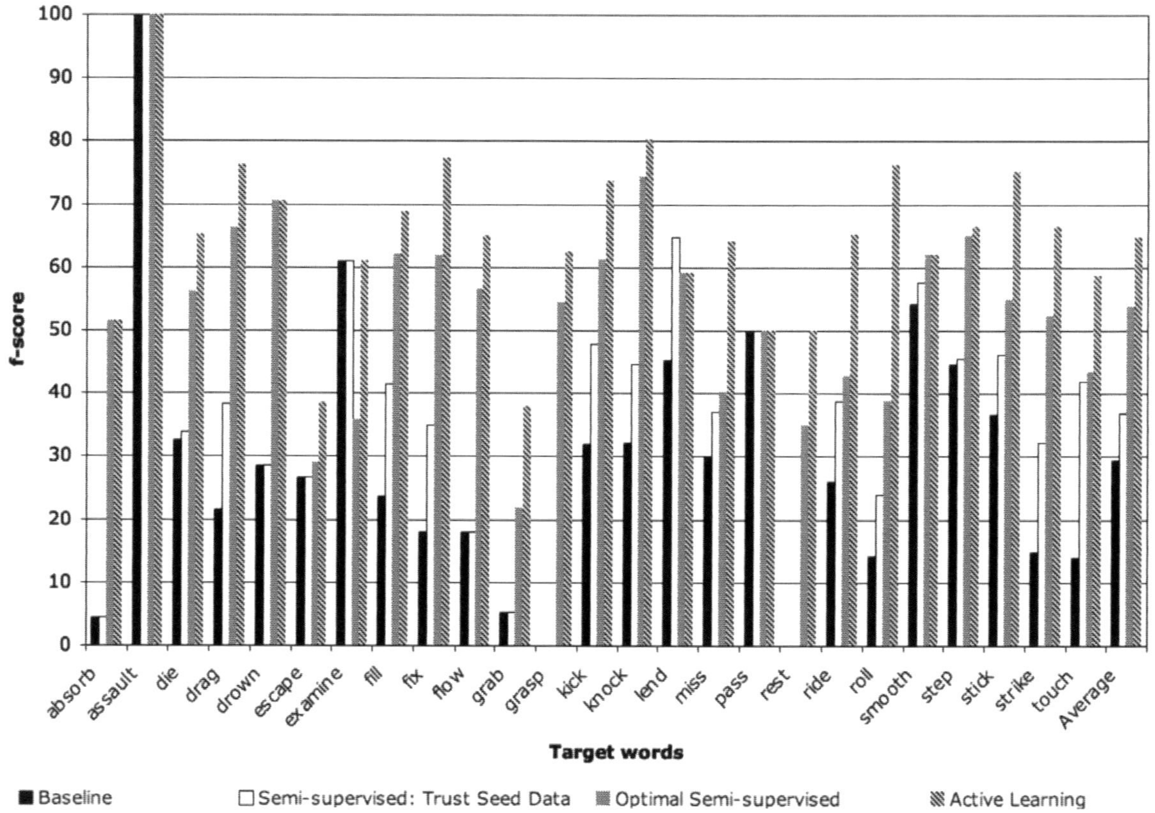

Figure 1: Active Learning evaluation results. *Baseline* refers to the second baseline from Section 2. *Semi-supervised: Trust Seed Data* refers to the standard KE model that trusts the seed data. *Optimal Semi-supervised* refers to the augmented KE model described in (Birke & Sarkar, 2006). *Active Learning* refers to the model proposed in this paper.

in an avarage f-score of nearly 36.9%. This is 23% higher than the 30% of the balanced case, which is 1.23 times higher. For this reason, we give the human scores a boost by assuming that whatever the human annotates in the manual scenario will result in an f-score that is 1.23 times higher. For our experiment, we take the number of sentences that our active learning method sent to the human for each word – note that this is not always 30% of the total number of sentences – and multiply that by 1.23 – to give the human the benefit of the doubt, so to speak. Still we find that using active learning gives us an avarage accuracy across all words of 64.9%, while we get only 21.7% with the manual process. This means that for the same human effort, using the weakly supervised classifier produced a three-fold improvement in accuracy. Looking at this conversely, this means that in order to obtain an accuracy of 64.9%, by a purely manual process, the human would have to classify nearly 53.6% of the sentences, as opposed to the 17.7% he needs to do using active learning. This is an effort-savings of about 35%. To conclude, we claim that our model combined with active learning is a helpful tool for a literal/nonliteral clustering project. It can save the human significant effort while still producing reasonable results.

4 Annotated corpus built using active learning

In this section we discuss the development of an annotated corpus of literal/nonliteral usages of verbs in context. First, we examine *iterative augmentation*. Then we discuss the structure and contents of the annotated corpus and the potential for expansion.

After an initial run for a particular target word, we have the cluster results plus a record of the feedback sets augmented with the newly clustered sentences.

pour
nonliteral cluster
wsj04:7878 N As manufacturers get bigger , they are likely to pour more money into the battle for shelf space , raising the ante for new players ./.
wsj25:3283 N Salsa and rap music pour out of the windows ./.
wsj06:300 U Investors hungering for safety and high yields are pouring record sums into single-premium , interest-earning annuities ./.
literal cluster
wsj59:3286 L Custom demands that cognac be poured from a freshly opened bottle ./.

Figure 2: Excerpt from our annotated corpus of literal/nonliteral usages of verbs in context.

Each feedback set sentence is saved with a *weight*, with newly clustered sentences receiving a weight of 1.0. Subsequent runs may be done to augment the initial clusters. For these runs, we use the the output identification over the examples from our initial run as feedback sets. New sentences for clustering are treated like a regular target set. Running the algorithm in this way produces new clusters and a re-weighted model augmented with newly clustered sentences. There can be as many runs as desired; hence *iterative augmentation*.

We used the iterative augmentation process to build a small annotated corpus consisting of the target words from Table 1, as well as another 25 words drawn from the examples of previously published work (see Section 5). It is important to note that in building the annotated corpus, we used the Active Learning component as described in this paper, which improved our average f-score from 53.8% to 64.9% on the original 25 target words, and we expect also improved performance on the remainder of the words in the annotated corpus.

An excerpt from the annotated corpus is shown in Figure 2. Each entry includes an ID number and a Nonliteral, Literal, or Unannotated tag. Annotations are from testing or from active learning during annotated corpus construction. The corpus is available at *http://www.cs.sfu.ca/∼anoop/students/jbirke/*. Further unsupervised expansion of the existing clusters as well as the production of additional clusters is a possibility.

5 Previous Work

To our knowledge there has not been any previous work done on taking a model for literal/nonliteral language and augmenting it with an active learning approach which allows human expert knowledge to become part of the learning process.

Our approach to active learning is similar to the Uncertainty Sampling approach of (Lewis & Gale, 1994) and (Fujii et. al., 1998) in that we pick those examples that we could not classify due to low confidence in the labeling at a particular point. We employ a resource-limited version in which only a small fixed sample is ever annotated by a human. Some of the criticisms leveled against uncertainty sampling and in favor of Committee-based sampling (Engelson & Dagan, 1996) (and see refs therein) do not apply in our case.

Our similarity measure is based on two views of sentence- and word-level similarity and hence we get an estimate of appropriate identification rather than just correct classification. As a result, by embedding an Uncertainty Sampling active learning model within a two-view clustering algorithm, we gain the same advantages as other uncertainty sampling methods obtain when used in bootstrapping methods (e.g. (Fujii et. al., 1998)). Other machine learning approaches that derive from optimal experiment design are not appropriate in our case because we do not yet have a strong predictive (or generative) model of the literal/nonliteral distinction.

Our machine learning model only does identification of verb usage as literal or nonliteral but it can be seen as a first step towards the use of machine learning for more sophisticated metaphor and metonymy processing tasks on larger text corpora. Rule-based systems – some using a type of interlingua (Russell, 1976); others using complicated networks and hierarchies often referred to as *metaphor maps* (e.g. (Fass, 1997; Martin, 1990; Martin, 1992) – must be largely hand-coded and generally work well on an enumerable set of metaphors or in limited domains. Dictionary-based systems use existing machine-readable dictionaries and path lengths between words as one of their primary sources for metaphor processing information (e.g. (Dolan, 1995)). Corpus-based systems primarily extract or learn the necessary metaphor-processing information from large corpora, thus avoiding the need for manual annotation or metaphor-map construction. Examples of such systems are (Murata et. al., 2000; Nissim & Markert, 2003; Mason, 2004).

Nissim & Markert (2003) approach metonymy resolution with machine learning methods, "which [exploit] the similarity between examples of conventional metonymy" ((Nissim & Markert, 2003), p. 56). They see metonymy resolution as a classification problem between the literal use of a word and a number of pre-defined metonymy types. They use similarities between *possibly metonymic words* (PMWs) and known metonymies as well as context similarities to classify the PMWs.

Mason (2004) presents CorMet, "a corpus-based system for discovering metaphorical mappings between concepts" ((Mason, 2004), p. 23). His system finds the selectional restrictions of given verbs in particular domains by statistical means. It then finds metaphorical mappings between domains based on these selectional preferences. By finding semantic differences between the selectional preferences, it can "articulate the higher-order structure of conceptual metaphors" ((Mason, 2004), p. 24), finding mappings like LIQUID→MONEY.

Metaphor processing has even been approached with connectionist systems storing world-knowledge as probabilistic dependencies (Narayanan, 1999).

6 Conclusion

In this paper we presented a system for separating literal and nonliteral usages of verbs through statistical word-sense disambiguation and clustering techniques. We used active learning to combine the predictions of this system with a human expert annotator in order to boost the overall accuracy of the system by 11.1%. We used the model together with active learning and iterative augmentation, to build an annotated corpus which is publicly available, and is a resource of literal/nonliteral usage clusters that we hope will be useful not only for future research in the field of nonliteral language processing, but also as training data for other statistical NLP tasks.

References

Srinivas Bangalore and Aravind K. Joshi. 1999. Supertagging: an approach to almost parsing. *Comput. Linguist.* 25, 2 (Jun. 1999), 237-265.

Julia Birke and Anoop Sarkar. 2006. In *Proceedings of the 11th Conference of the European Chapter of the Association for Computational Linguistics, EACL-2006*. Trento, Italy. April 3-7.

Barbara Di Eugenio and Michael Glass. 2004. The kappa statistic: a second look. *Comput. Linguist.* 30, 1 (Mar. 2004), 95-101.

William B. Dolan. 1995. Metaphor as an emergent property of machine-readable dictionaries. In Proceedings of Representation and Acquisition of Lexical Knowledge: Polysemy, Ambiguity, and Generativity (March 1995, Stanford University, CA). AAAI 1995 Spring Symposium Series, 27-29.

Sean P. Engelson and Ido Dagan. 1996. In *Proc. of 34th Meeting of the ACL*. 319–326.

Dan Fass. 1997. *Processing metonymy and metaphor*. Greenwich, CT: Ablex Publishing Corporation.

Atsushi Fujii, Takenobu Tokunaga, Kentaro Inui and Hozumi Tanaka. 1998. Selective sampling for example-based word sense disambiguation. *Comput. Linguist.* 24, 4 (Dec. 1998), 573–597.

Yael Karov and Shimon Edelman. 1998. Similarity-based word sense disambiguation. *Comput. Linguist.* 24, 1 (Mar. 1998), 41-59.

David D. Lewis and William A. Gale. 1994. A sequential algorithm for training text classifiers. In *Proc. of SIGIR-94*.

James H. Martin. 1990. *A computational model of metaphor interpretation*. Toronto, ON: Academic Press, Inc.

James H. Martin. 1992. Computer understanding of conventional metaphoric language. *Cognitive Science* 16, 2 (1992), 233-270.

Zachary J. Mason. 2004. CorMet: a computational, corpus-based conventional metaphor extraction system. *Comput. Linguist.* 30, 1 (Mar. 2004), 23-44.

Masaki Murata, Qing Ma, Atsumu Yamamoto, and Hitoshi Isahara. 2000. Metonymy interpretation using *x no y* examples. In *Proceedings of SNLP2000* (Chiang Mai, Thailand, 10 May 2000).

Srini Narayanan. 1999. Moving right along: a computational model of metaphoric reasoning about events. In *Proceedings of the 16th National Conference on Artificial Intelligence and the 11th IAAI Conference* (Orlando, US, 1999). 121-127.

Malvina Nissim and Katja Markert. 2003. Syntactic features and word similarity for supervised metonymy resolution. In *Proceedings of the 41st Annual Meeting of the Association for Computational Linguistics* (ACL-03) (Sapporo, Japan, 2003). 56-63.

Adwait Ratnaparkhi. 1996. A maximum entropy part-of-speech tagger. In *Proceedings of the Empirical Methods in Natural Language Processing Conference* (University of Pennsylvania, May 17-18 1996).

Sylvia W. Russell. 1976. Computer understanding of metaphorically used verbs. *American Journal of Computational Linguistics*, Microfiche 44.